SOCIETY
TODAY 2

Patrick McNeill

M
MACMILLAN

First published 1991

Published by
MACMILLAN EDUCATION LTD
Houndmills, Basingstoke, Hampshire RG21 2XS
and London
Companies and representatives
throughout the world

Printed in Hong Kong

British Library Cataloguing in Publication Data
McNeill, Patrick
Society today 2 — (Macmillan sociology).
1. Great Britain. Sociological perspectives
I. Title   II. New Society   III. New Statesman and Society
301.0941
ISBN 0–333–54108–1

Contents

Preface

The articles in this book are a selection from all those published between September 1987 and March 1990 in the series 'Society Today', which initially appeared in *New Society* and then in *New Statesman and Society*.

The series followed another of the same title but a different format, which was edited by Michael Williams in *New Society*. The collected edition of that series was published by Macmillan in 1986 with the title *Society Today*.

I would like particularly to thank David Lipsey, formerly editor of *New Society*, for giving me the chance to edit and write this series of articles. His guidance and support for the first few months of the series was essential to whatever success it has had.

The demands of producing a piece every week in term-time are very great, and I would like also to thank Tony Cole, the most regular of my 'guest' writers, for producing high quality pieces on time whenever he has been asked to do so.

Thanks too are due to the sociologists who agreed to be interviewed for the articles which appear in this volume as Articles 60 to 66, 68 and 69.

Patrick McNeill
April 1990

Acknowledgements

Article 2,   'Creating Disasters' is by Roger Gomm.
Article 4,   'Theory of Welfare' is by Tony Cole.
Article 5,   'The Impact of Television' is by David Barrat.
Article 16,   'Football Hooliganism' is by Tony Cole.
Article 32,   'A Good Judge?' is by Tony Cole.
Article 40,   'Citizens' Rights' is by Chris Brown.
Article 42,   'Accidents can Happen' is by Tony Cole.
Article 43,   'The Green Light' is by Peter de la Cour.
Article 46,   'Moving Houses' is by Tony Cole.
Article 54,   'Hate Attack' is by David Cutler and Karim Murji.

Patrick McNeill and the publishers wish to thank these contributors for
their co-operation in providing permission to use copyright material.

Part I
Society Today

1

The Core Curriculum

How and Why is it Chosen?

In July 1987 Kenneth Baker, the Secretary of State for education, published proposals to introduce a core curriculum in schools. He wants pupils between eleven and 16 to be taught three core subjects: maths, English and science. They would take up between 30 and 40 per cent of the pupils' timetable. Seven other subjects (a modern foreign language, technology, history, geography, art, music and physical education) should take up perhaps 50 per cent of the remaining time, leaving somewhere between 10 and 20 per cent of the timetable for everything else, including religious education. Many topics such as health education and careers advice can, Baker suggests, be taught through other subjects.

Sociologists' interest in the school curriculum dates mainly from the publication in 1971 of Michael Young's book *Knowledge and Control*. Drawing on the sociology of knowledge, this book argued that the school curriculum should be treated as problematic. Since it is not self-evident what should be included in it, it is necessary to explain just what is, and why.

The school curriculum is the result of a process involving the *production, selection and ranking* of knowledge. When this knowledge has been *transmitted*, pupils are *assessed* on their ability to demonstrate what they have learned.

The sociology of knowledge originates in the work of Marx, Mannheim and the phenomenological philosophers of the first half of this century. It challenges the common-sense view that knowledge is true for all times and all places, and aims to show that it is closely tied to its social context. It stresses that knowledge is produced and used socially, and that it is *relative* to its context. Furthermore, knowledge is often used in the interests of the particular group who have it, who may be in a position to withhold it from others.

Irrelevant to and useless in everyday life

Practical knowledge ◄────────► Abstract knowledge

Relevant to and useful in everyday life

Figure 1

The view that derives from Marx emphasises that knowledge is essentially *ideological*, in that it can be used to maintain or change the social structure. At any particular period in history, the dominant ideas are designed to promote the stability of society and thus serve the interests of those in power.

How does this insight apply to Baker's core curriculum? It stresses that how knowledge is organised and classified into subjects is a social process. The subject matter of chemistry, physics and biology do not exist separately in the natural world, and there is nothing to determine that science has to be taught under these specialist headings. So why *is* knowledge learned in schools carved up into 'subjects'?

Then, there is the question of *selection*. Obviously, only a part of all knowledge can be included in the curriculum. How is this selection made? By whom? And why is specialisation so important?

Selection also occurs within a subject. Who decides which aspects of biology will be included, and how do they choose? In history, for example, why was the emphasis traditionally on political history, on kings and queens and battles? What caused the move in the 1970s towards more social and economic history, and towards the examination of original sources?

A 1987 paper from the (Tory) Centre for Policy Studies states that: 'the quality of history taught in schools continues to decline. A new philosophy holds that since nothing is ultimately knowable and records are inevitably biased, the evaluation of sources is far more important than any learning of facts . . . GCSE syllabuses no longer teach pupils about our national heritage in an orderly fashion . . . if at all'.

Will this challenge to the modern teaching of history be successful? Will the core curriculum restore 'facts' to the classrooms?

The point to stress is that curriculum choices are made by those with power, who decide what is appropriate knowledge for school pupils of various ages and abilities. When this selection has been made, and the curriculum fixed, different subjects have different status. In Baker's scheme, maths, English and science are the core. But why should this be so? What criteria has he used?

You might like to complete the diagram shown in Figure 1. List the subjects that you are studying, or have studied, and place them in position on the grid. Take woodwork as an example. This is relevant to and useful in everyday life, so it belongs in the lower half of the grid. Much of it is practical knowledge, so it belongs on the left-hand side. Overall, it will therefore be somewhere in the box at bottom left. A level English literature, by contrast, is not so obviously relevant to or useful in everyday life, and is very abstract, so it goes somewhere in the top right-hand corner of the grid.

When you have placed several subjects, including sociology, in the school curriculum, identify which quarter of the grid contains the high status subjects, the ones that you can take at A level and for a degree, and which ones people admire you for being good at. Are they the more or the less everyday, the more or the less abstract? Are they mainly 'head' or 'hand' knowledge? What is the significance of the pattern that emerges?

The curriculum, like education as a whole, is a deeply political issue. It is political in the sense that there is disagreement about whether there should be a centrally imposed curriculum at all, and there is lively disagreement about what should be included in it. This will be resolved through political debate and through the exercise of power, and in a way that will be approved by the powerful.

Basil Bernstein sums up the argument: 'How a society selects, classifies, distributes, transmits and evaluates the educational knowledge it considers to be public, reflects both the distribution of power and the principles of social control'.

2 OCTOBER 1987

FURTHER READING

Ball, S. (1986) *Education* (Longman).

Reid, I. (1986) *The Sociology of School and Education* (Fontana) pp. 68 – 76.

And, for the much more advanced:

Bernstein, B. (1971) 'On the Classification and Framing of Educational Knowledge', in M.F.D. Young, *Knowledge and Control* (Collier Macmillan).

2

Creating Disasters

The Unequal Impact of Natural Disasters

'In Hertford, Hereford and Hampshire, hurricanes hardly ever happen'. But typhoons, hurricanes, cyclones, blizzards, droughts, floods and earthquakes occur relatively frequently in other parts of the world, particularly the third world, where loss of life and damage to property can be on an enormous scale.

However, it is important not to assume that the severity of a natural disaster is directly related to the severity of natural phenomena in terms of measurements such as windspeeds. What makes a natural disaster disastrous is the vulnerability of the people it affects. Poor people in poor countries are much more vulnerable to the effects of natural phenomena than are people in affluent nations.

In October 1987, a hurricane struck southern England. There was extensive damage to property; travel and communications were disrupted, and normal economic activity was brought to a temporary halt.

As a result of the storm, 17 people died. However, it is unlikely that the death rate for southern England for that day was greatly increased. For those who died because of the storm, there were others who did not die because they did not travel on the roads or face the hazards of the workplace. In terms of deaths, this 'natural disaster' was a minor affair, compared to those in the third world.

For example, in 1974 Cyclone Tracy seriously damaged the town of Darwin in Australia causing 49 deaths. Within 18 months the damage was repaired and Darwin was functioning much as before. In the same year, a hurricane of similar force hit the coast of Honduras. It caused 8000 deaths, and some of the devastation persists 13 years later.

Such differences have to be understood in social, political, and economic terms. In Honduras, peasant farmers had been dispossessed from the coastal plain by large American fruit companies and had begun to clear the forests from the mountain sides. Once the forest was removed, the soil became unstable. The hurricane caused landslides which killed many people, and flooding, which killed many more. Large tracts of the country were rendered totally uncultivatable.

This process of marginalisation, whereby people are forced into ever more dangerous situations, is what makes disasters in the third world so disastrous. Third world governments often promote marginalisation in the quest for higher export earnings.

They encourage the felling of forests, the building of dams vulnerable to earthquakes, the irrigation of unsuitable lands, and the dispossession of peasants by agribusiness corporations. In this they are aided and abetted by the large multinational corporations. The south-east of England is, in fact, one of the largest concentrations of shareholders in multinational corporations in the world.

The economies of whole countries are also more or less vulnerable to disaster. A third world country dependent on the export of a few agricultural commodities is much more vulnerable to the effects of a natural disaster than a country with a diverse industrial and agricultural economy where a disaster is less likely to damage the entirety of its export-earning capacity.

Rich countries have far greater resources for dealing with disaster. After the 'killer storm' in south-east England, most roads were cleared within hours and most of the injured had received good medical treatment. Within days most of the railway lines were back in operation and power restored to almost all areas cut off. By the following Monday, very few workplaces remained closed. Within weeks, most of the damaged buildings will have been repaired.

A prosperous region like southern England has enormous resources for coping: emergency services; capital equipment like helicopters, cranes, pumps and vehicles; and complex social organisations which can be turned to cope with disasters.

Much has been made of the cost of the gales, which has been cited in hundreds of millions of pounds. More important than the amount, though, is the way in which the costs are shared. In England, all but those who are too poor or too feckless to fully insure their property are likely to be compensated. The cost will be spread thinly among everyone insured in the form of higher premiums. The costs of emergency services, of medical treatment, of repairs to roads and public buildings will likewise be spread out through taxation. The costs will be socialised.

There are gainers as well as losers. There will be financial cost to some companies because of lost production, but many of their workers will gain from overtime opportunities. Construction plant hire companies, glaziers, and companies making building components, and their workers, are likely to gain from the disaster. In the short term, the gales may even cause a fall in levels of unemployment.

In a third world country, by contrast, most people are too poor to insure against loss. Government services and administrative systems are on a small scale and poorly resourced, because in a poor country tax revenues are low. There will be a shortage of medical facilities and of capital equipment because these expensive industrial products have to be bought from abroad.

In such circumstances, the risks faced by individuals can neither be spread through the private sector by insurance nor through the public sector by taxation. The effects of a disaster are likely to be borne fully by those most directly affected: the peasant whose land is washed into the river, the householder whose house is blown away. While a disaster may sometimes create short-term work for the workless, it is much more likely that it will create higher unemployment because of shortages of resources necessary for reconstruction.

Looking at 'natural' disasters helps us to see an important facet of inequality which is often ignored in discussions of income, wealth, power and prestige: security. Natural disasters may strike at random, but their effects are largely determined by the wealth, income and power of individuals and nations, and the way in which societies are organised to share the burden of disaster.

6 NOVEMBER 1987

Discussion Topic

Personal disasters are like natural disasters. Discuss the ways in which poor people in Britain are more vulnerable to illness and accident.

FURTHER READING

Wijkman, A. and Timberlake, L. (1984) *Natural Disasters: acts of God or acts of man?* (London: Earthscan).

3

The Moral Society

Moral Judgements and the Sick

'Everywhere I go, I see increasing evidence of people swirling about in a human cesspit of their own making . . . ' James Anderton, chief constable of Greater Manchester, speaking last year about the spread of AIDS, assumed a clear causal link between AIDS and what he regarded as immoral behaviour.

Many people reacted angrily to Anderton, rejecting his belief that AIDS is some kind of divine retribution for wrongdoing, and his reference to homosexual acts as 'obnoxious practices'. But while the way that Anderton linked disease and morality was offensive to many, there is often an implied moral judgement about the victims of disease.

In the past, and in contemporary cultures less dominated by western notions of science, the link between ill-health and moral responsibility has often been pronounced. The biblical plagues of Egypt, for example, were seen as God's punishment for evil-doing. Attempts to cure the sick through exorcism reflect a belief that possession by devils is the root cause of disease.

With the rise of scientific medicine in the 19th century, the perceived link between evil and illness was weakened, as more objective causes were identified. For example, when the incidence of cholera in London was shown to be related to the location of water supplies, the supplies were cleaned up and cholera was brought under control. No blame was attached to victims.

Orthodox modern medicine operates largely in accordance with a biomechanical model. Ill-health occurs when the body is invaded from outside by some agency (bacteria, viruses and so on), and the practice of medicine concentrates on destroying these external agents.

The emphasis is on curing disease after it has occurred. The model focuses on the body as a machine which may break down or malfunction. No moral judgement is implied about the owner of this defective machine, who is not normally held responsible for its breakdown.

This view has been increasingly challenged by various types of alternative medicine, which emphasise the link between mind and body, but most general practitioners, and virtually all hospitals, operate in terms of the biomechanical model.

Even within this model, the question of moral responsibility for disease is not straightforward. Certain diseases are perceived as being linked to lifestyles, and so to some extent under the control of the individual. With the growing emphasis on preventative rather than curative medicine, greater responsibility for being ill is placed on the individual sufferer.

A recent example of change in the moral status of a disease is provided by lung cancer. Smokers who develop lung cancer will still be treated, but perhaps with less sympathy than a non-smoker.

With the advent of 'healthy eating' and low fat diets, anyone who is seen knowingly to persist in eating fried foods, saturated fats and so on, may be regarded as 'having only themselves to blame' if they develop heart disease. If they are also a heavy smoker, they may receive even less attention.

With constraints on health service resources, may it become necessary to base decisions about who receives treatment on such considerations? Will 'innocent victims' be given priority over those who are seen to be ill through their own fault?

AIDS, associated as it is in the public mind with homosexuality and illegal drug use, is just the latest example of this linking of morality and disease. With the press playing an active role, AIDS has become the centre of a moral panic in which attitudes and beliefs about health, disease, morality, sexuality and responsibility have become tightly interwoven.

Peter Aggleton and Hilary Homans (1987), as part of their research into education about AIDS, distinguish between professional and lay (non-professional) explanations of the disease. Professional medical opinion maintains that AIDS is caused by a virus (HIV), which can be transmitted between people in a limited number of very specific ways.

Lay opinion, however, has various explanations. Some people believe that AIDS is caused by homosexuality itself. Another view is that some people have an inborn predisposition towards developing AIDS. Others believe that it is highly contagious, and can be caught by sharing eating or washing utensils. Yet others maintain that the disease spreads through the air, and that certain locations are more dangerous than others. All these are essentially physiological theories, but several have clear moral undertones.

Aggleton and Homans have also identified various 'personal responsibility' theories of the disease, and found that people distinguish between innocent and guilty victims. 'Innocent' victims include haemophiliacs, children, and the spouses of unfaithful partners. 'Guilty' victims include gay men, prostitutes and intravenous drug users.

These theories feature widely in press reports, and clearly link blameworthiness with the breaking of social and moral norms.

Lastly, there are the lay theories, exemplified in Anderton's remarks, which see AIDS as divine retribution for immoral behaviour.

To hold someone responsible for their own disease is to make a moral judgement about their life style. To make such a judgement is the first step towards claiming the right to control certain kinds of behaviour in certain groups.

Viewed in this way, medicine involves not only the practice of science, but also the exercise of power.

'In the modern world, all too often there is no clear line between concern for the welfare of others and coercive control of their lives. A new kind of power relationship has arisen in society. Authorities who understand our bodies have gained the right to make and enforce rules about morality.' (Foucault)

20 NOVEMBER 1987

Discussion Topic

Make a list of about a dozen illnesses or disorders (include mental illnesses, if you wish).

Consider each in turn.

Under what circumstances might someone be held responsible for contracting it?

FURTHER READING

Aggleton, P. and Homans, H. (1987) *Educating for AIDS* (NHS Training Authority).

Hart, N. (1985) *The Sociology of Health and Medicine* (Causeway Press).

Kennedy, I. (1981) *The Unmasking of Medicine* (Allen & Unwin).

4

Theory of Welfare

What is the Role of the Welfare State?

According to John Moore, Secretary of State for Social Services, human happiness is enhanced by government policies that help people 'to be independent, to use their talents, to take care of their families and to achieve things on their own'. (Speech quoted in The *Guardian*, 2 October 1987.)

Moore is responsible for guiding through parliament legislation which will reform the welfare state more drastically than at any time since the immediate postwar period. Like education, health, and housing, social security is about to undergo its biggest changes for 40 years.

Naturally enough, the underlying philosophy of the reforms echoes that expressed by Moore. He has a clear view of how much the state should do for its citizens and how much they should do for themselves. His remarks deliberately reject the sort of approach to welfare which dominated British politics from the 1940s to the 1960s and which represented a consensus between the main political parties.

The central core of that consensus was the belief in the state's responsibility for the welfare of its citizens. This belief drew heavily on the work of two key thinkers. One was the economist, John Maynard Keynes (1883–1946), who argued that high levels of unemployment such as those experienced in the 1930s, could and should be overcome by government economic policies.

The other was William Beveridge (1879–1963), whose report published in 1942 formed the basis of the postwar package of welfare reforms. Central to this report was an emphasis on welfare as a form of citizenship, expressed through the benefits, available to all, of the national insurance scheme and the system of family allowances.

Both writers were firmly committed to capitalism; both were very wary of what they saw as excessive state power. But both felt that government intervention in the economy was necessary if economic slumps and poverty were to be avoided. For these reasons, they have been called 'reluctant collectivists' (George and Wilding, 1976).

The Fabian socialist tradition also fed into this consensus, via its influence on the Labour Party. This view, dating from the early years of this century, stressed the importance of the role of government in building a more equal society. Unlike marxists, who argue for socialism 'from below' by revolutionary working-class struggle, Fabians advocate a more gradual road to social and economic reform through state action from above.

Moore's opposition to this consensus is illustrated by his description of its vision as being 'of a huge, benevolent, all-embracing, all-providing state, taking control of citizens' lives'. 'Under the guise of compassion' he says, 'people's confidence and will to help themselves was undermined'.

Moore's views represent what George and Wilding call an anti-collectivist ideology, which is associated with Mrs Thatcher's years as leader of the Conservative Party. Though these views are now advocated by the so-called New Right, they stem from the 19th-century ideology of *laissez-faire*, of which there are three main elements.

The first element is the belief that the economy works best without government intervention or regulation. For example, governments should avoid laying down minimum wages because this prevents wages 'finding their own level' through the laws of supply and demand. In 1986 all minimum wage protection for workers under 21 was abolished.

The second element is the belief in the individual's right and ability to look after his or her own social and economic well-being. There are two assumptions underlying this belief: one is that problems like poverty and unemployment can be solved by the individuals concerned; the other is that people are freer when they provide for themselves, such as by buying their own education or health care.

The third element of *laissez-faire* is the argument that welfare provision is more efficient when bought by the individual in the marketplace. This is because the providers of these services then have to compete with each other to attract the consumer.

What implications does this anti-collectivist ideology have for the social security system? A central feature of Moore's view is the belief that the postwar consensus led to the 'indiscriminate handing out of benefits', which undermined self-help, reduced resources available for those 'in real distress', and caused resentment among tax-payers who paid for this allegedly easy money.

As a result, he advocates a much greater emphasis on targeting benefits so as to ensure that they go only to those in real need. Since the 1940s, there has, in practice, been a drift towards targeting through the use of means-tested benefits. This drift has now become a conscious and deliberate policy.

Critics of means-testing point to the low rate of take-up for such benefits as supplementary benefit, housing benefit and family income supplement. They also point to the way that people lose their entitlement to many benefits as their income from employment rises, sometimes ending up little better off (the poverty trap). Other critics note how tax allowances, such as that on mortgage interest payments, go to all income tax payers, regardless of their income and without a means test. They therefore tend to favour the better-off.

This article has taken up the points raised by a study of Moore's speech, particularly his individualist critique of the postwar welfare consensus. A full discussion of the ideologies of welfare, however, would have also to look at other perspectives. It would have to explore the feminist critique of the way that much welfare policy is based on assumptions of male dominance and female domesticity and dependency.

It would need also to look at the marxist analysis of the role of welfare in reinforcing capitalist inequality (Cole, 1986). Nor should it be forgotten that the Conservative tradition of Tory paternalism, a residue of a kind of aristocratic concern for the poor, still lingers in some parts of that party.

27 NOVEMBER 1987

Discussion Topic

Take child benefit as your example:
● Find out how much is payable and to whom.
● What might feminists say about it and why?

FURTHER READING

Cole, T. (1986) *Whose Welfare?* (Tavistock).

George, V. and Wilding, P. (1976) *Ideology and Social Welfare* (Routledge & Kegan Paul).

5

The Impact of Television

Does TV Violence Influence Viewers?

These are troubled times for British television. Accusations of left-wing bias made by leading Tories like Norman Tebbit have brought a promise from BBC Deputy Director-General, John Birt, of 'more polite' political interviewing. The murders in Hungerford and in Bristol have triggered a new moral panic. And, once again, television stands accused by the popular press of being the cause of violence . . . this time in the form of 'Rambo-style' killings.

The Sun, reporting the shooting of four people in Bristol, went straight to the heart of the matter. They interviewed the owner of the local video store, who was reported to say of the accused man: 'Usually he came in on a Saturday night and asked if we had any good "action movies"'. 'He liked lots of violence and particularly liked Clint Eastwood and Rambo . . . in fact, any film with Sylvester Stallone'.

Should social scientists draw conclusions about the effects of the media from such awful events? Even psychologist Hans Eysenck, who believes that television is a major cause of social violence, agrees that a strong case cannot be based on isolated incidents. Rigorous laboratory experiments, he claims, can provide the only valid evidence.

Sociologists are unlikely to share Eysenck's faith in experiments. But they would agree that case studies, however horrific and newsworthy, are unreliable evidence. If we forget that, then we commit ourselves to censorship on a massive scale. It would be a bit like banning baths because murderers have used them to drown their victims.

The logic of such an argument would lead to 'cleaning up' not only television and film but also other fictional forms – books, plays and poetry. And it is difficult to see how factual descriptions of real-life events – news and documentary reports of events like the Enniskillen bomb – could be excluded from this censorship.

There is a long history of people blaming the media for social ills. At various times, the criticism has focused on comics, on films, and even on popular theatre. Critics of the media see the issue as a matter of common sense. Certain television programmes are 'obviously harmful' and the solution is simple; reduce the 'excessive violence'.

But, when media researchers have tried to produce a working definition of 'excessive violence', they have experienced enormous difficulties. For one thing, our response as viewers depends on the context in which the violence occurs. Is it an understandable part of an unfolding tale? Does it occur in a cartoon, in a news story, or in a soap opera?

During the summer of 1982, the *Daily Mail* ran a hard-hitting series of articles on 'video nasties'. To catch the eye of the reader they used a drawing of a child watching television with rapt attention. On the screen was the image of a devil. The message was of helpless innocence at the mercy of irresistible forces of corruption.

The *Daily Mail* logo and the *Sun* account of a crazed killer in a hungry search for video violence both contain a germ of truth. Television does influence our lives, our thoughts, our knowledge, our dreams and our feelings. The error lies in supposing that the process of influence is simple and direct. We are, on the one hand, passive recipients of a one-way communication. But we are also active consumers of media products, browsing, selecting, and rejecting according to our tastes. Recently, media sociologists have thrown some light on the act of consumption which is known as 'watching television'.

What does 'watching television' mean? Only rarely are we fully attentive consumers. Psychologist Peter Collett videoed families while they watched television, by installing a hidden camera in their sets. It revealed that people do many different things while they are 'watching television'. They range from close attention to apparent unawareness that the set was even on. Many aspects of family life occur in front of a switched-on television set. According to Collett, people talk, eat, sleep, iron, read, knit, kiss, argue, do homework and vacuum the carpet.

This observation, obvious as it may seem, throws new light on statistics which show, for instance, that children spend more time watching TV than they do in school, or that the average adult watches more than 30 hours of television a week. It also suggests that we should find out more about how television is consumed if we are to understand its effects.

Unlike a magazine or a personal stereo, television is a medium often consumed in family groups. It may have a number of functions which are linked more closely to family life than to the medium itself.

Television may be used as a barrier to communication, turned on 'because I don't want to talk to anyone'. At other times we may agree to watch a programme to please someone else. It is also sometimes used as a scapegoat, a mediator, a boundary marker between family members (sport for men, soaps for women, children's television), to schedule activities ('Let's go to bed after *News at Ten*'), as a reward ('You can watch *X* if you finish your homework first'), as a punishment ('No television tonight'), and as a bartering tool ('You can watch *Top of the Pops* so long as you do the washing up/clean your bedroom/apologise to your sister').

Morley, in a series of in-depth interviews with 18 London families, was struck by the role of gender relations in television consumption. In most of the families he studied, programme choice was under male control (father or son). Remote controls were male possessions, sometimes even taken away when the male left the room. Men had a single-minded and serious approach, consulting schedules and watching attentively.

But the wives' domestic obligations made such dedicated viewing a rare and guilty luxury. It is clear from such work that an understanding of family relationships is one of the essentials if we are to unravel the effects of the media on their audiences.

4 DECEMBER 1987

Discussion Topic

What is 'excessive violence'? How might this be defined in a way that a sociologist could use in research?

FURTHER READING

Collett, P. and Lamb, A. (1985) *Watching People Watching Television* (unpublished report to the IBA).

Eysenck, H. and Nias, D. (1980) *Sex, Violence and the Media* (Paladin).

Morley, D. (1986) *Family Television* (Comedia).

6

Christmas Rituals

The Exchange of Gifts

'There's only eleven shopping days to Christmas'. Though rituals exist in all societies, Christmas is the most ritualised annual event in our calendar. The Christmas ritual most apparent to an outside observer must be the giving of presents.

Rituals are formal actions, following a set pattern, which are primarily symbolic. Anthropologists have shown that a set of actions may be 'instrumental' (that is, the intention and effect is to get something done), or it may be 'expressive' (its purpose lies in what it says symbolically, in the values that it expresses).

Some actions involve both elements. An example of an instrumental action might be to catch a bus to work. An expressive action would be to wave to somebody from the window of the bus. An action that is instrumental *and* expressive would be always to meet a colleague at the bus-stop and to go to work together in order to arrive at the same time.

At Christmas, most people give presents to people from whom they expect to receive a present in return; it is an exchange. Such ritualised gift exchanges are found in many societies. Two of the best-known examples are the Kula ring, and the Potlatch.

In the former, described by Malinowski (1922), two kinds of article (necklaces of red shell and bracelets of white shell) are continuously circulated in opposite directions round the islands of the Trobriand group, being exchanged for the article circulating in the other direction, under highly ritualised conditions. No individual retains possession of an item for any length of time.

On the face of it, Kula is a futile activity, though it does have, albeit indirectly, the instrumental function that, alongside the Kula exchanges, ordinary trade and barter is carried on. However, the Kula valuables are, in themselves, useless. It is their expressive function that is the key to understanding this gift-exchange ritual. The exchanges confer prestige on those who participate, and symbolise the reciprocity which sustains this scattered society.

The Potlatch of the Kwakiutl of the northwest of America and Canada was first described at the end of the nineteenth century. It was essentially a party, often to mark a special occasion like a marriage, or a peace-making, which included the giving of gifts to all the guests. The prestige gained by the chiefs who gave these parties depended on their generosity, and a record was kept of who gave what. The receivers then had to respond and would lose face if they were less generous.

The new-found opulence of the Kwakiutl at the start of this century, combined with their traditional competitiveness, led to a rapidly spiralling increase in the extravagance of the Potlatch, reaching a climax in parties where huge quantities of goods, many of real value, were burned, smashed, and thrown into the sea in demonstrations of 'conspicuous consumption'. While the early Potlatch may have had some instrumental function in distributing goods among the tribal groups, the later displays were entirely concerned with expressing power and prestige.

Sociologists since Durkheim, and such anthropologists as Radcliffe-Brown in the 1920s, have emphasised the importance of expressive ritual for integrating social groups. They argue that rituals express important social values, such as the need for solidarity between members of a group or community. By repeating relatively rigid and stereotyped patterns of behaviour which, in themselves, serve no purpose, people intensify their fellow-feeling as members of a group.

In our society, the exchange of gifts at Christmas can be interpreted in similar ways. Gift-exchange helps, for example, to sustain family relationships and friendships, especially over long distances. The value (not necessarily monetary) of gifts reflects the value the giver attaches to the relationship, and also the status of the partners in the exchange.

A gift which is unsuitably generous may be intended to symbolise the giver's wish to create or to develop a relationship, but may merely arouse suspicion. A gift which is perceived as mean will arouse resentment. If no reciprocal gift is forthcoming at all, a snub may be both intended and recognised, or unintended but nevertheless felt. Receiving an unexpected present puts pressure on us to give a present in return, which maybe we cannot afford or do not want to give. But to fail to respond may have more symbolic meaning than we would wish.

An expensive but frivolous present may have greater expressive value than a sensibly-priced but 'useful' (instrumental) one. The comparison between giving someone Marks & Spencer underwear or Janet Reger lingerie illustrates the point nicely. Lovers may give each other large pink cuddly toys, but are unlikely to give each other socks.

As in the Potlatch, wealthy people give extravagant parties where they may give expensive presents to relative strangers. Some private companies do the same for their business contacts. In this case, the exchange element is less direct and implies both thanks for past custom and the expectation of its continuing. The whiff of bribery may even be in the air.

There are also echoes of the Kula ring in our system. We do not circulate exactly the same objects round such a ritualised circuit, but by the time enough people have given each other the same kind of mass-produced objects (bath soap, ties, bottles of sherry) the final effect is much the same. What adult has never been given a present virtually identical to one they had given to some third party?

Through the giving of Christmas presents, we create and reinforce family, social, political and business relationships. We may repair broken relationships, or prevent enmities developing. There may be a more or less conscious attempt to exhibit superior wealth and power. It is on these symbolic meanings of the gift exchange that advertisers base their appeals to us to spend, spend, spend at Christmas time.

11 DECEMBER 1987

Discussion Topic

Describe the rules for sending Christmas cards as though you were explaining them to a visiting anthropologist.

FURTHER READING

Lewis, I.M. (1976) *Social Anthropology in Perspective* (Pelican).

Malinowski, B. (1922) *Argonauts of the Western Pacific* (RKP).

7

Is Religion Declining?

How can we Measure Religious Activity?

On Christmas Eve, our local free newspaper carried advertisements for religious services at the Parish Church (Church of England), the Methodist Church, the Baptist Church, the Catholic Church, the Evangelical Church, the Free Evangelical Baptist Church, the Marley Chapel and the United Reformed Church.

This list does not exhaust the total of Christian religious organisations in a middle-sized English town. And it ignores the many other religions represented; Muslim, Hindu, Sikh, Buddhist, Jewish, and others. It would appear, on this evidence at least, that religion still plays an important role in many people's lives.

The established church, too, seems to be of abiding interest, at least to the media. In December, 1987 there was the fuss made about the introduction to the *Crockford's Directory*, which anonymously attacked the supposedly progressive attitudes of the Archbishop of Canterbury. The author of that introduction was hunted down, and subsequently found dead. Then, in the week after Christmas, the tabloid headlines announced that the Bishop of Ripon had banned practising homosexuals from being trained or ordained. The interest taken in these events greatly outweighed the number of people directly affected.

A contrasting news item over the holiday period was provided by a report from Save Britain's Heritage, which stated that in the last 18 years 1115 of Britain's 15,000 Anglican churches have been lost to worship. Of these, a quarter have been demolished. In addition, the Methodist Church has lost half its 14,000 chapels since the war. On this kind of evidence, religious practice would seem to be in decline.

So what is happening to religion in Britain today? Has the secularisation process, described by Wilson (1966) as 'the process whereby religious thinking, practice and institutions lose social significance', continued unabated? Or are things more complicated than that? And what would be evidence for or against religious decline?

As far as numbers are concerned, the overall picture appears to be that 'while congregations in the established Christian denominations dwindle, an evangelical revival is taking place outside the framework of conventionally organised formal worship. And non-Christian religions are on the up-and-up' (*New Society*, 20 December 1985). Thus, for example, while the numbers and the percentages of Anglicans and Roman Catholics continued to decline from the mid-1970s to the present, the number of Mormons, Jehovah's Witnesses, and Spiritualists grew steadily, and the House Church movement grew from nothing to involving nearly 200,000 people today.

In addition, the number of Muslims more than doubled (to over 800,000). Sikhs and Hindus also increased in number, and the number of people in non-Christian churches grew to over one and a half million by 1985.

In simple numerical terms, then, the process of secularisation appears not to be taking place. Even for the traditional churches, though the number of people attending them once a week has declined since Victorian times, their membership peaked in the 1960s, and today has fallen back no further than Victorian levels.

But the main focus of interest in the sociology of religion in recent years has been on the rapid growth in the numbers and membership of New Religious Movements (NRMs), such as the Unification Church (the Moonies), Scientology, and Hare Krishna, as well as the Mormons and Evangelicals mentioned above. Many of these sects and cults provide a certainty, even a dogmatism, of beliefs that many people find attractive. This appears to lend weight to Durkheim's thesis, developed by Robert Merton, that a rapidly-changing society becomes anomic, losing its foundation of shared values and beliefs, and that people will then seek out some alternative moral base.

As the traditional churches become more liberal and progressive, so some people feel compelled to find more conservative, even reactionary, belief systems on which to base their lives. Seen in this way, the right-wing political revival and the growth of the evangelical movement, especially in the USA, is not coincidental.

In a recent book, in which he looks at religions world-wide, Nelson refers to an 'outburst of religiosity unique in human history'. He maintains that sociology, in concentrating on people's material and social needs, has lost sight of their spiritual nature. He explains the growth of NRMS in terms of human beings looking for new ways of satisfying their spiritual needs.

In taking a close look at the many non-church varieties of religious observance, he argues that traditional churches are in fact the enemy of religious creativity. There is, he says, a historical cycle in which authentic religious and spiritual experience degenerates into church religion. It is only when the grip of the churches weakens, as it has done in this country in recent years, that people 'can escape the control of the organisation and are able to make personal contact with God'. Only then can religious creativity flourish. Secularisation, Nelson believes, has reached its limits and the religious tide is turning.

So where does this leave religion in Britain today? Has the supposedly steady process of secularisation been reversed? Or was it, in fact, never as widespread as some sociologists thought?

Perhaps a way through these apparent contradictions is to make a distinction between the role of religious belief in people's lives, and the role of the established church in society as a whole. After all, many people have argued that schools are anti-educational. Might not the established churches be anti-religious?

8 JANUARY 1988

Discussion Topic

This article has identified only a very few points which relate to the question of secularisation. What other evidence could be used to assess the importance of religion in Britain today?

FURTHER READING

Nelson, G.K. (1978) *Cults, New Religions and Religious Creativity* (Routledge & Kegan Paul).

Wallis, R. (1984) *The Elementary Forms of the New Religious Life* (Routledge & Kegan Paul).

Wilson, B. (1966) *Religion in a Secular Society* (C.A. Watts).

8
Understanding Language

| Is Language Neutral? |

David Alton's bill to amend the Abortion Act, 1967, had its second reading in the House of Commons in January 1988. The bill proposed that the limit after which an abortion is illegal should be reduced from 28 weeks to 18 weeks. Most of the public discussion of the bill was centred on the moral issues involved, but the language in which this debate had been conducted prompted considerations of interest to the sociologists.

Indeed, to note the language used by anyone involved is the quickest way to identify which side of the argument they are on. To talk of 'terminating a pregnancy' or 'doing an abortion' rather than 'killing a baby' is to do more than just choose words. It is an attempt to structure the listener's perception of the situation in such a way that they will interpret it as the speaker does, and so come to share their moral stance.

In common-sense terms, if we think about it at all, we tend to assume that words are labels that we attach to objects in the world so that we can communicate with each other about them. For example, the world includes objects which we call 'dog', the French call 'chien' and the Italians call 'cane'. We assume that there is an objective reality, already divided into categories, which we use words and language to describe.

Philosophers of language, particularly those influenced by the later writings of Wittgenstein, would turn this idea on its head. They maintain that it is the structure of language that conditions how we think about the world and, therefore, how we perceive it. As John Searle expressed it in a recent television discussion:

'The structure of our language determines the way we think of the real world. It determines what we count as one object or two objects or the same object; it determines what we count as an object at all. We cannot discuss the world and we cannot even think of the world independently of some conceptual apparatus that we can use for that purpose. And, of course, the apparatus is provided by language.' (Magee, 1987)

Wittgenstein's view was developed in the sociological context by Edward Sapir and his student, Benjamin Whorf, whence it has become known as the Whorfian hypothesis.

Since the structure of a language conditions the way a speaker of that language perceives reality, people who speak the same language will tend to share a perception of reality. This perception is different from people who speak other languages. As Sapir put it:

'No two languages are ever sufficiently similar to be considered as representing the same social reality. The worlds in which different societies live are distinct worlds, not merely the same worlds with different labels attached.'

If this is so, then language is an important, if not the most important, influence binding a society or any other social group together. This group cohesion can operate at various levels. In schools, for example, though teachers and pupils share the same basic language, each group, especially pupils, will use words and phrases in special ways that exclude from the group anyone who does not share that meaning. A teacher who tries to share in the slang of the playground is trying to close the social gap between themselves and pupils, and will usually not get very far.

At the level of nation states, wars and civil conflict have been linked with language loyalties, as in the case of French in Canada, or Flemish in Belgium. The Welsh Nationalists place great emphasis on the retention and revival of the Welsh language. In Gwynedd, Welsh is the first language in schools, even when the child's first language may be English.

For language is more than a medium of communication. It is more than a means of ensuring social bonding. It is also a way of exercising power, whether in the interests of maintaining the status quo, or of changing it.

One of the first things the countries of Africa did when they regained their independence was to restore their mother-tongue names. Thus Rhodesia, so named in the 19th century after the British colonialist Cecil Rhodes, became Zimbabwe.

Similarly, the city of Derry in Northern Ireland was renamed Londonderry several centuries ago after the London merchants who controlled it. To call it Derry today is to demonstrate a nationalist political allegiance. As a TV journalist has said:

'The words you use may betray the political path you seem to be treading. Where is the conflict taking place? Is it in Ulster? Northern Ireland? The Province? The North of Ireland? Or the Six Counties? And once you've sorted out the names, what is actually going on there? Is it a conflict? Is it a war? A rebellion? A revolution? A criminal conspiracy? Or a liberation struggle? Are those involved terrorists? The mafia? Murderers? Guerrillas? Or freedom fighters?'

Dale Spender and others have applied the argument to the feminist debate. Sue Lees (1986) shows how the term 'slag' is used by teenagers as a form of social control. To be termed a slag is something to be avoided. The way to avoid it is to enter into a steady relationship with a boy at the earliest opportunity, and to follow that relationship into marriage.

Crucially, the acceptance and use of particular words in particular contexts legitimates particular forms of conduct. If freedom fighters are terrorists, they can be shot or imprisoned. If fetuses are babies, it becomes much harder to justify carrying out abortions. In fact, the words 'killing babies' make it impossible to justify the action. It is possible, however, to argue in favour of 'terminating a pregnancy'.

Whoever wins the war of words will legitimate their approach to the problem, for it is their interpretation of the situation which will be embodied in the law.

22 JANUARY 1988

Discussion Topic

Various words are used to refer to old people who live in residential homes: inmates, patients, residents, clients.
How do these words relate to our expectations of how they should be treated?

FURTHER READING

Lees, S. (1986) *Losing Out* (Hutchinson).

Magee, B. (1987) *The Great Philosophers* (BBC Books; 1987).

Spender, D. (1980) *Man-made Language* (Routledge & Kegan Paul).

9

The Objectivity of Statistics

Official Statistics

The publication of the 1988 edition of *Social Trends* was, as usual, the signal for the 'serious' newspapers to regale their readers with what they considered to be the more newsworthy snippets of information contained therein. The headlines on household spending power, the gap between the rich and poor and on AIDS show what the journalists thought was newsworthy in the 220 pages. The social scientist, while also welcoming this annual publication as a treasure-trove of statistical information, has other interests in the material.

The Government Statistical Service, which produces *Social Trends*, is responsible for the collection and publication of all official statistics, which cover a vast range of social, political and economic activity. The data it provides is usually regarded as objective and reliable, a statistical portrait of Britain.

The cover of the 1988 *Social Trends* makes the point neatly. There are three snapshots, each showing a family group. One is from before the First World War, one from about the late 1950s, and one is contemporary. These pictures appear to 'speak for themselves'. We are invited, implicitly, to see the contents of *Social Trends* as a similar kind of record of social life in Britain. But it takes no great insight to recognise that these photographs are posed, that their subjects are selected and that everything outside the frame of the picture is unknown and unknowable to us. The person who took the picture controls what we see. What we should recognise is that the same is true of official statistics.

Social statistics are a form of social knowledge. Like all knowledge, they are the result of generative procedures. That is to say, knowledge is not just lying about waiting to be collected, but is created through routine processes. In the case of official statistics, we can ask how they are created, why and by whom. We could also consider how they are presented, and how they are used.

Official statistics are created in several ways. Some are the outcome of social surveys, of which the best-known example is the Census, carried out every ten years since 1801 (except for 1941). Other state surveys include the *General Household Survey* and the *Family Expenditure Survey*. Many official statistics are derived from registration procedures, such as those of birth, marriage and death. Some, like most statistics on the economy, are the result of returns made, either automatically or on demand, by employers and others.

And why are these statistics created? Historically, the earliest Censuses were carried out by rulers, usually to help them calculate potential tax revenues, or military resources. The *Domesday Book* is the obvious example. In England in the 16th century, mortality statistics were collected, and it was shown for the first time that there are regularities and patterns in death. This knowledge was used, among other things, to launch the life insurance industry.

Today, the orthodox reason put forward to explain and justify the mass of statistical returns that are required by government is that they make possible long-term social and economic planning, as well as enabling the evaluation of the results of government policies. The implication is that these statistics are needed and used by government for essentially benevolent purposes.

Thus, knowing how many babies have been born makes it possible to plan primary school provision for five years' time. In another example, the 1988 edition of *Social Trends* revealed how the number of one-person households is increasing steadily, which gives some indication of housing needs for the future. The figures for increasing life-expectancy suggest that the health of the nation has improved, the credit for which might be claimed by the public health authorities and by the health service.

This view of an essentially benevolent state is challenged by marxist analysts, who argue that, since the state is an instrument whereby the dominant class maintains its power, statistics collected by the state must necessarily contribute to this process. Official statistics are not only created, but are created in particular ways to further particular interests. The primary purpose of statistics, seen in this way, is to enable the bureaucratic state to control the people.

In addition, by judiciously selecting which statistics will be created and which will not, let alone their presentation, the state can legitimate its activities. Statistical knowledge thus contributes to the dominant ideology.

This view is not held only by marxists. At present, the issue of an 'ethnic question' in the Census is being discussed. Since the 1971 Census, attempts have been made to ascertain how many members of the ethnic minorities are resident in Britain, where they live and what their social and economic status is. For this to be known, the Census form would have to include a question which asks people directly what their ethnic origin is.

Besides the difficulties of wording such a question, many people are concerned about the use to which such data would be put. If the state is seen as essentially impartial, then its claim that the information would be used for the benefit of the ethnic minorities can be believed. But if the state is seen as fundamentally racist, then this data is seen to be offering opportunities for control and regulation, to the disadvantage of members of the minorities.

As Martin Slattery (1986) puts it:

'All forms of social knowledge represent power: the power to inform or mislead, the power to illuminate or manipulate. Whoever controls the definition of official statistics controls what is collected and how much; whoever controls the interpretation of official statistics controls public debate (and criticism); whoever has the power to withhold official data (or not collect it in the first place) has the power to prevent public discussion from arising.'

29 JANUARY 1988

Discussion Topic

Look through, say, four recent editions of your daily newspaper. Identify every occasion on which an 'official statistic' is cited. Consider how the information quoted might be used to benefit the group concerned, and then how it might be used against them.

FURTHER READING

CSO (1988) *Social Trends 18* (HMSO).

Irvine, J. (1979) *et al. Demystifying Official Statistics* (Pluto Press).

Slattery, M. (1986) *Official Statistics* (Tavistock).

10
Party Politics in Democracy

Politics and Pluralism

Seldom, if ever, have the affairs of a political party, let alone two political parties, been conducted as publicly as the negotiations between the Liberals and the Social Democrats. The wheeling and dealing throw a good deal of light on the reality of party politics in Britain.

The problems faced by Steel and Maclennan were the result, at least in part, of the nature of political parties and their role in our system of government. Parties are a key element of this system, which most commentators would describe as democratic. 'Democracy' is a term whose meaning has changed since it was first developed by the ancient Greeks. For them, democracy meant literally 'rule by the people'. Key political decisions were made on the basis of a vote taken in public by all citizens. (It is worth noting, in passing, that the system was not *that* democratic: citizens with the right to vote did not include women or slaves.)

In the modern world, democracy has come to mean 'representative democracy', a system in which the people elect representatives, to whom they pass the right to make laws and social policy, usually through the medium of a parliament. Political elites exist. But they are seen not as the enemies of democracy but as an integral and necessary part of it. A variety of elite groups compete for power. What keeps the process democratic is that these elites are open to new members and are accountable to those who elect them.

Whereas in the Greek system the citizens controlled government policy directly, in representative (or 'liberal') democracy this control becomes indirect. It is exercised through a system of accountability, which requires governments, at regular intervals, to offer the electorate the chance to re-elect them or to elect an alternative government.

Those who believe that Britain enjoys such a system of liberal democracy are 'pluralists'. Examples are Robert Dahl and Jean Blondel. They believe that political power in this country is not the monopoly of any single group, but instead is dispersed through a variety of groups among which none is supreme. The role of the state is to act as a neutral 'honest broker' between competing groups, provided that they all observe the proper rules of political discourse and activity. Political decisions are usually the result of compromise between these competing groups, which include political parties and pressure groups, who maintain a basic consensus about the justice of the system itself.

A pluralist analysis places particular emphasis on the role of political parties and of pressure groups. Pressure groups are organisations which try, through a wide variety of means, to influence the decisions of government, whether at national or local level. They may do this on particular issues, when they are called 'promotional' groups. Or they may try to defend the interests of a particular group of people. They are then known as 'sectional' groups. Examples of promotional groups would include Shelter, the Hunt Saboteurs and the National Viewers and Listeners Association. Examples of sectional groups include trade unions, the Confederation of British Industry and the British Medical Association.

Political parties, rather than trying merely to influence governments, aim to form a government by contesting and winning elections. They organise around a group of more or less loosely related issues. They aim to bind together into a single electoral force a group of people who, while sharing certain basic political beliefs, also have divergent interests in particular policies.

Parties have to aggregate a wide range of such interests if they are to become large enough to have any real chance of forming a government. This is why the major parties have left and right wings, and why all parties are, from time to time, threatened with a split. This is not to say that pressure groups never have splits, but theirs are usually over means rather than ends.

What we have witnessed in the Liberal and SDP merger talks is an attempt to aggregate a set of policies which will enable the two parties to merge and contest elections as one. It has been the obverse of avoiding a split.

The Liberal Party and the SDP aim to occupy the middle ground of British politics, between what they see as the growing extremism of right and left. The root of Steel and Maclennan's difficulties has been to design policies which are acceptable to people with widely varying political views. They have tried to create a balance in their domestic policies by allowing market forces to operate while at the same time giving the state powers to limit the undesirable effects of those forces. The aim is to attract the left wing of the Conservative Party and the right wing of Labour into a central party which will 'break the mould' of the two-party system.

A two-party system is one in which only two parties are in a position to compete for an absolute majority of seats. They can, therefore, make a credible claim to be a potential party of government, without needing to form a coalition. Consequently, the norm is that government alternates between these two parties. This system has dominated British politics since the Second World War. However, there was a period in the late 1960s and at the 1974 and 1983 elections when a multi-party system seemed possible. Some commentators suggest that a single-party system is now developing.

Besides any lack of political appeal that the minor parties may suffer from, the British voting system, at both local and national level, makes it particularly difficult for a third party to make any headway at elections. The 'first-past-the-post' voting systems means that a third party may win a far larger percentage of votes than seats in parliament. Despite winning 22.6 per cent of the United Kingdom votes at the 1987 election, the Alliance won only 22 of the 650 seats.

Even if the merger goes through successfully, and even if the new party can produce a set of agreed policies which have widespread appeal, there is still the problem of making an electoral breakthrough in a system which is positively unhelpful to such an initiative.

5 FEBRUARY 1988

Discussion Topic

This discussion has been entirely within a pluralist framework. What criticisms have been made of this approach?

FURTHER READING

Ball, A. (1987) *British Political Parties* (Macmillan).

Bottomore, T. (1979) *Political Sociology* (Hutchinson).

11

Strikes and Society

Explaining Industrial Conflict

Health service workers (including some nurses) on strike: the Ford strike going ahead in the end; the pit deputies (NACODS) having their first-ever national strike; the National Union of Seamen in dispute over the Isle of Man ferries. This sudden flurry of industrial disputes is almost reminiscent of the 1970s, when the number of working days lost through strikes was far higher than now. With occasional 'blips', the overall trend in the number of working days lost through industrial disputes since the late 1970s has been downward.

Industrial conflict is expressed in many different ways, of which strikes are only one. In its less organised forms, conflict and dissatisfaction among employees can be apparent in low morale, pilfering, high rates of absenteeism and of staff turn-over and sometimes through acts of sabotage. Where workers are more organised, overtime bans, go-slows and working to rule are forms of conflict that fall short of strike action. A strike is, as Hyman (1984) makes clear, a *temporary stoppage* of work, undertaken *collectively* by a group of *employees*, who have usually *calculated* that their action will help to express their grievance or enforce their demands.

Sociological explanations of industrial conflict have changed substantially in the last 15 years, in line with changing perspectives on the nature of work in a capitalist society and thus of the employer/employee relationship.

The simplest view of this relationship is sometimes called the 'unitary' view, and assumes that the interests of organisation, employer and employees are the same. Trade unions are not allowed in the workplace because they are seen by management and owner to have no relevance. Strikes are wholly unacceptable, and rare, since the workers have little or no opportunity to organise.

More widely held today is the 'pluralist' view, which recognises a basic conflict of interest in the employer/employee relationship, and acknowledges the value of setting up representative organisations (such as trade unions) and negotiating machinery to ensure that any potential conflict is defused. All sides agree to abide by formal rules of negotiation and to be bound by whatever is agreed after consultations. Conflict is thus institutionalised, and strikes are seen as evidence of the breakdown of these arrangements. Critics of this view point out that the basic distribution of power is still the same. 'Management still commands: workers are still obliged to obey' (Hyman, 1984).

The sociology of industrial relations now argues that both the unitary and the pluralist perspectives are defective. This is because they view industrial relations in isolation from the wider political and economic structures of capitalist society. This wider view has its origins in the work of Marx, but its recent development starts with Braverman (1974). He focuses on the labour process, on 'any organised system of activity whereby the human capacity to produce results in a useful article or service' (Horne, 1987), and argues that the nature and the experience of work changes with changing social and economic conditions.

Those who have developed Braverman's argument, often in a critical response to it, stress that the employer/employee relationship involves both conflict and co-operation. While it is true that capitalists are in the business of exploiting their employees, and ultimately have power over them, they also need their co-operation. And while workers of course seek to maximise their earnings, it is also in their interests to keep the business successful.

How workers and managers respond to this tension between co-operation and conflict varies from one situation to another, but always within the wider economic and political context of the times.

During the late seventies and the eighties, the economic context has been one of recession, and the political context has seen a related decline in the power of the trade unions. After attempts by both Labour and Conservative governments of the 1970s to limit the power of the unions, Mrs Thatcher's strategy of what Hyman calls 'coercive pacification' seems to have had the effect she wanted.

Government policies since 1979 have deliberately increased unemployment with the result that membership of the trade unions has fallen, and employers have been more able to hold down wage increases, to lay off workers and to increase productivity, as there has always been the threat of the dole queue. A series of laws restricting union power, particularly in the context of industrial disputes, has had a more direct effect. The Employment Act, 1980, outlawed secondary picketing; the Employment Act, 1982, enforced secret ballots for the closed shop, and the 1984 act, possibly the most significant, requires unions to hold secret ballots before taking strike action.

Seen in this way, an explanation of strikes must take into account the immediate work situation, the perceptions of those involved, and the wider context of capitalism. Strikes are not incidental breakdowns in the work situation, but part of the labour process. Industrial relations are part of a system that goes far beyond the workplace, and increasingly involves the state. Certainly, the strike of the miners in 1984/85 was about much more than wages and working conditions. As was made clear by the NUM throughout the strike, they saw themselves as fighting to save their jobs and their communities.

The action of the nurses, while aimed primarily at securing a wage increase, is also a protest at public spending cuts which they regard as calculated to damage the national health service beyond recall. Recent strikes by teachers and other public sector workers have also had this double thrust: the desire both for a wage increase and to save public services from government policies, including privatisation, which are weakening or destroying them.

12 FEBRUARY 1988

Discussion Topic

'It is even less possible than previously to treat strikes as an isolated social phenomenon: they can only be understood within a broader political economy of industrial relations.' (Hyman, 1984) How far do you agree with this statement?

FURTHER READING

Braverman, H. (1974) *Labour and Monopoly Capital* (Monthly Review Press).

Horne, J. (1987) *Work and Unemployment* (Longman).

Hyman, R. (1984) *Strikes* (Fontana).

12

Comic Relief and Aid

Who Really Benefits from Foreign Aid?

So Comic Relief raised ten million pounds for the third world. The TV comedians followed Band Aid, Live Aid and Sport Aid in contributing to the huge sums that have been collected by voluntary effort since the Ethiopian famine appeared on our TV screens in 1984.

The word 'aid' conjures up an image of unselfish giving, with no advantage to the giver and great benefits for the receiver. The motives of Comic Relief were certainly altruistic, but is the reality of aid to the third world so simple?

Wealth flows from the rich countries of the world into the third world in several ways, not all of which can be called aid. Foster-Carter identifies five such flows. First, military aid, which is not intended to aid development, but involves huge sums.

Second, direct investment by foreign companies in third world countries, perhaps by building factories or buying agricultural land. This is done for commercial rather than altruistic reasons, and so is not aid as such. Some would argue that any capital flowing into the third world must be a good thing, in that it creates jobs and incomes. Others maintain that the huge multinational companies making these investments acquire too much political influence in the countries concerned, and that in any case the profits are channelled back to shareholders in the wealthy countries, rather than reinvested in the third world.

The third flow is private loans from Western banks, charged at commercial interest rates. This gives third world countries a greater say in how the money is used, but the problem is that, as debts grow and interest rates rise, a point is reached where virtually all the income of the debtor country goes on paying interest charges, let alone repaying any of the original loan.

Fourth is voluntary aid. This is where Comic Relief comes in. The major agencies through which such aid is channelled include Oxfam and Save the Children. But their efforts are tiny in comparison with Official Development Assistance, though often more cost-effective.

The fifth type is Official Development Assistance (ODA), which is 'aid' in the strict sense and refers to grants or loans whose main purpose is development or welfare, rather than direct profit. Interest is charged on loans at less than the commercial rate. Such aid may be given by one country to another (bilateral) or via one of the international agencies, such as the World Bank or the International Monetary Fund (multi-lateral).

A country granting bilateral aid will often make a condition that the recipient spends the money buying products from the donor country. This is called 'tied aid' and about 70 per cent of British bilateral aid (which totalled £847 million in 1986) is on these terms, which creates a lucrative market for British manufacturers.

A further criticism of ODA is that it is used by wealthy countries, particularly the two superpowers, to exercise political influence in third world countries, and to support political regimes, however corrupt, which are friendly towards the donor country. The USA, in particular, has never made any secret of using aid as a political weapon.

ODA is a post-colonial phenomenon, with its origins in the period after the Second World War which saw the last of the great European empires and the winning of political independence by many third world countries. Initially, aid was seen primarily as a way of helping such countries to buy the imported goods they needed to stimulate their economies into growth.

In the event, growth was less than anticipated and, when the world economy entered a period of instability in the early seventies, many poorer countries resolved their short-term difficulties by borrowing money at the going rate of interest. With the rise in interest rates of the eighties, the debt problem became a crisis. The point has now been reached where this burden of debt makes it impossible for some third world countries to develop, as any capital growth they achieve flows back to the north as interest payments.

But even before the crisis of the eighties, there were challenges to the orthodox view that aid was the answer to the problems of the third world. The Brandt Report of 1980 argued that, while aid should be doubled in the short term, this should be with a view to developing international trade in the long term. The wealthy countries of the north should gear production to the needs of the poorer south, who, in their turn, should supply raw materials to the north. Restraints on international trade should be minimised, so that, by trading with each other, each group of countries could help itself while also helping the other. Third world countries should have a greater say in the decisions of the IMF and the World Bank.

But much more fundamental criticisms than this have been made.

From the right of the political spectrum, Bauer argues that aid, far from helping economic development in the third world, is an obstacle to progress because it discourages enterprise. In Bauer's view, economic growth, both national and international, can only come through encouraging the free market.

The mechanisms of the market will ensure that capital finds its way to where it can be most profitably invested to stimulate further growth. The third world is poor, he argues, because it has failed to provide the conditions to attract commercial investment. The very concept of a 'third world' is a myth created and sustained by foreign aid.

Hayter's analysis comes from the opposite end of the political spectrum. She has called aid 'the smooth face of imperialism', and regards it as no more than a continuation of the exploitation of the third world that originated in the colonial era. Aid, especially tied aid, provides 'leverage' which enables the north to dominate the economies of the south in ways which favour capitalism. She is particularly critical of the policies of the IMF, whose conditions for loans, she argues, actively increase the dependency of third world countries.

While no one could find moral fault with Comic Relief's wish to save lives, aid and development involve much more complex issues.

26 FEBRUARY 1988

Discussion Topic

What, if any, was the real value of Comic Relief?

FURTHER READING

Foster-Carter, A. (1987) 'Development', in *Developments in Sociology*, Vol. 3 (Causeway).

Webster, A. (1990) *Introduction to the Sociology of Development* (Macmillan).

13

Defining the Poor

How Can We Measure Poverty?

In April 1988, the most wide-ranging reforms of social security for years were implemented. They are the latest link in a chain which goes back to the social welfare legislation enacted between 1900 and the First World War.

The existence of poverty has been acknowledged by the state at least since Elizabethan times, and there have been various attempts to devise a scale to identify those eligible for benefit. One of the earliest was the Speenhamland decision of 1795, which linked allowances to changes in bread prices. But only in the last 100 years have social scientists been involved in attempts to define poverty scientifically and measure its extent accurately.

Charles Booth spent 16 years on inquiries which led to the publication between 1889 and 1903, in 17 volumes, of his *Life and Labour of the People in London*. He asked 'who are the poor?' and 'why are they poor?' To answer these questions required a definition of poverty. In his own words:

'The divisions indicated here by "poor" and "very poor" are necessarily arbitrary. By the word "poor" I mean to describe those who have a sufficiently regular though bare income, such as 18 shillings (£0.90) to 21 shillings (£1.05) per week for a moderate family, and by "very poor" those who from any cause fall much below this standard. The "poor" are those whose means may be sufficient, but are barely sufficient, for decent independent life; the "very poor" those whose means are insufficient for this according to the usual standard of life in this country.'

He found 30.7 per cent of London's population living below this standard. This supported his later advocacy of an old age pension of five shillings (£0.25) per week. The scheme introduced by Lloyd George's government in 1908–9 owed a great deal to Booth's work.

Booth's younger contemporary, Seebohm Rowntree, took the study of poverty further, drawing up the first precise scale of poverty, covering a variety of family size and circumstance. In his study of York, published in 1901, Rowntree was careful to define poverty in a way that could not be criticised as being too generous. Using what has been called the 'budget standards approach', he consulted experts about basic dietary and other needs, and costed these carefully. He wrote:

'Families regarded as living in poverty were grouped under two heads: (a) families whose total earnings were insufficient to obtain the minimum necessaries for the maintenance of merely physical efficiency. Poverty falling under this head was described as "primary poverty"; (b) families whose total earnings would have been sufficient for the maintenance of merely physical efficiency, were it not that some portion of it was absorbed by other expenditure, either useful or wasteful. Poverty falling under this head was described as "secondary poverty".'

Rowntree's category of secondary poverty has often been misunderstood, for it does *not* only mean poverty that could be avoided if people managed their affairs more sensibly. It means poverty that results from buying anything other than that 'which is absolutely necessary for the maintenance of physical health'. He found 10 per cent of York's population in primary poverty and 18 per cent in secondary.

The importance of Rowntree's early work is that it set the pattern for official scales of poverty to the present. Sir William Beveridge, whose 1942 report was the basis of the welfare legislation after the Second World War, calculated the level at which benefits should be paid by referring to Rowntree's 'human needs' scale, revised in 1937, and adding the cost of rent. Beveridge stressed 'my primary poverty line was a bare standard of subsistence rather than living . . . such a minimum does not by any means constitute a reasonable living wage'. Beveridge favoured the idea of universal benefits, disliking means-testing on principle.

The Rowntree/Beveridge approach underpinned the introduction of national assistance (later to be replaced by supplementary benefit and now by income support) except in the way that means-testing has become more widely used. It is in these tests that the major source of disagreement arises. As the new DHSS fact sheet says:

'The amount of income support a person can get depends mainly on how much the law says they need to live on, and how much money they already have coming in from things like other social security benefits and part-time work.'

The scales are revised annually, but no one could reasonably describe them as generous, and many people on benefit describe their lives as 'existing rather than living'. In recent years sociologists have studied this difference. After writers like Titmuss as early as the 1950s, Peter Townsend and others have argued that poverty should be measured not only in terms of basic material needs, but also in terms of the quality of life, in relation to that of others in the community. This is often called a 'relative' measure of poverty.

'People must have an income which enables them to participate in the life of the community. They must be able, for example, to keep themselves reasonably fed, and well enough dressed to maintain their self-respect and to attend interviews for jobs with confidence. Their homes must be reasonably warm; their children should not feel shamed by the quality of their clothing; the family must be able to visit relatives, and give them something on their birthdays and at Christmas time; they must be able to read newspapers, and retain their television sets and their membership of trade unions and churches. And they must be able to live in a way which ensures, so far as possible, that public officials, doctors, teachers, landlords and others treat them with the courtesy due to every member of the community.' (Donnison, 1982)

Attempts to quantify the poverty line in these terms have been central to sociological studies since the 1960s, but they seem to have had little impact on the sums paid in income support.

15 APRIL 1988

Discussion Topic

Obtain a set of the *Reforming Social Security* fact sheets, free from 20–24 Lonsdale Road, London NW6 6RD. What assumptions about poverty are implied in them?

FURTHER READING

Donnison, D. (1982) *The Politics of Poverty* (Martin Robertson).
Thane, P. (1982) *The Foundations of the Welfare State* (Longman).

14

Teachers and Unions

Are Teachers Professionals?

The main teachers' unions held their annual conferences over Easter 1988 and several modified their policies towards the government in similar ways. For example, the National Union of Teachers, the largest union, voted against a policy of non-compliance with the new Education Act and established an 'Independent Education Commission' to monitor its introduction. This decision contrasts markedly with the NUT's recent, more combative responses to government policy.

The change has been greeted as a 'new realism', but the vote at Scarborough is significant at a deeper level. It can be seen as another phase in the history of teachers' struggle to increase their power as an occupational group.

All occupational groups devise strategies to try to improve their position in the labour market and the conditions under which they offer their labour to clients and employers. By combining into organisations, they seek to improve their power and thus to improve their financial rewards and their status, as well as their autonomy in the work situation.

The two major such strategies are trade unionism and professionalism. Many occupations have made a clear choice between these strategies (for example, the miners for trade unionism, solicitors for professionalism) but others, such as nurses, local government officers and teachers seem to vacillate between the two, or even try both.

A key characteristic of a profession is the existence of a professional association, such as the British Medical Association, the Royal Institute of British Architects or the Law Society. These protect the market situation of their members in various ways. A central strategy is to control the supply of labour into the profession, by ensuring that only those who have passed the qualifying examinations set by the association can practise.

The professional association also takes responsibility for the quality of the performance of its members, and has powers to discipline members or to strike them off the register. The fact that being struck off tends to happen more readily to members who have brought the profession into disrepute than to those who have been incompetent suggests that the association is about protecting the reputation of its members, more than the safety or security of clients. Professional associations also conduct or sponsor research.

When trade unions perform these functions, it may be perceived in a very different way. Thus, the professionals' protection of clients by ensuring that only the properly qualified carry out the work becomes the trade unions' closed shop, and is effectively outlawed. The rule whereby solicitors cannot appear for their clients in the crown court becomes a restrictive practice when one craftsman refuses to carry out the work of another. Some professional restrictive practices and monopolies, such as conveyancing by solicitors, have been recently identified as such and abolished, weakening the market situation of solicitors.

Overall, however, occupations which have successfully established professional associations are in a stronger market situation than those who have followed a trade union strategy, and much stronger than those which are not unionised.

In the case of teachers, it is not for the want of trying that they have never attained full professional standing. Parry and Parry (1974) suggest an explanation for this failure, and make a comparison with doctors. In the 19th century, both groups made efforts to improve their market situation. Teachers, assisted by the establishment of training colleges in the 1840s, set up the College of Preceptors in 1846, but its scope was limited.

Doctors were more successful. The Medical Registration Act, 1858, established the General Medical Council and created the legal monopoly that ensured the subsequent power of the profession. At this point, neither occupation was employed by the state.

Parry and Parry argue that, once the state adopted a major role in the provision of schooling from 1870 onwards, and became the main employer of teachers, it was against the state's interests to allow teachers the professional independence achieved by doctors. A series of efforts to establish a Registration Council for Teachers, in 1869, 1879, 1881 and 1890, all foundered in parliament.

Despite repeated efforts in the 20th century to establish a register which would enable them to control entry to the occupation, teachers have in practice relied on the NUT (founded in 1870) and other unions to improve their status and hence their market situation. Besides their work on teachers' pay and conditions, the unions have been involved in many aspects of educational policy, which have improved both the quality and quantity of education and also improved the standing of teaching as an occupation.

In the area of training, for example, there has been steady progress. The length of training was increased in the early 1960s from two to three years. This was followed by the introduction of the four-year B.Ed. degree and the move towards all-graduate entry. This brought teacher training closer to the elite sector of higher education and so to the established professions. Despite this, there are still many unqualified teachers in schools and colleges, so the ultimate position whereby only qualified persons are legally permitted to practise is still denied to teachers.

In the Parrys' view, the state's success in preventing the professionalisation of teachers has been helped by the internal divisions of occupation. It is divided by the status of subjects, by the age group of pupils, by gender differences, by religious differences, and by the existence of the private sector. In addition, teachers have not established an exclusive body of knowledge, as have doctors and lawyers.

Given the lack of success of professionalism as an occupation strategy for teachers, they turned to increasingly militant unionism in the 1960s and 1970s. Could it be that the relative failure of this strategy in the eighties has led to teachers turning again to professionalism?

29 APRIL 1988

Discussion Topic

Using the ideas in this article, consider whether nurses are best served by a trade union or a professional association.

FURTHER READING

Parry, N. and Parry, J. (1974) '*The Teachers and Professionalism*', in M. Flude and J. Ahier, *Educability, Schools and Ideology* (Croom Helm).

15
In and Out of Work

What Exactly is Work?

As the monthly unemployment figures continue their downward trend, the headlines tell us that there are fewer people 'out of work'. Leaving aside the question of how far the unemployment statistics have been manipulated to produce this impression, the idea of being 'in work' or 'out of work' is worth a closer look.

For many years, the sociology of work identified work with paid employment. The sociological stereotype of the worker was the wage-labourer in manufacturing industry, together with the white-collar (black-coated?) office worker.

In the last 20 years, the reduction in the proportion of people working in manufacturing industry, the growth of the service sector, greater unemployment, more women in paid employment, the success of feminist sociology in showing that domestic labour is work, the growth in leisure opportunities: all these changes have prompted sociologists to re-examine their narrow understanding of work.

In an important article first published in *New Society* in 1980, Gershuny and Pahl distinguished between the formal and the informal economy. The formal economy is that which is measured by economists as contributing to the Gross National Product, and is essentially what both everyday common sense and traditional sociology recognise as work. There have been changes in patterns of working in the formal economy, especially in the 1980s, with increases in self-employment, part-time employment, flexitime working, and working from or at home.

The informal economy, said Gershuny and Pahl, has three elements; the household economy, the hidden or black economy, and the communal economy. Gershuny and Pahl no longer accept some of the points they made in 1980, and later writers have modified their threefold classification.

For example, Deem (1988), drawing on Finnegan (1985), in Open University course DE325, identifies three aspects of the hidden economy. First there is the illegal work done by the professional burglar or the drug-dealer. None of these activities are normally thought of as work and, as they are illegal, it is impossible to fully estimate their extent. But they all result in material gain, and involve time and effort, as well as risk.

The second element in the hidden economy is work whose proceeds are not declared to the taxman or any state authority. Such work is not in itself illegal, and may be done to augment a main income. It is done by some as a second job, by others while they receive a pension or benefit, and by some, like married women, as their sole source of independent income.

The third element in the hidden economy involves pilfering from employers and exploiting the perks of a job, such as an expense account. Such activities are not so important in considering the sociology of work, but they are certainly a source of gain (and of cost to the employer).

Deem further subdivides the informal economy between domestic work and work in the community. Until very recently, the work which takes place, mostly unpaid, in private households has been largely unrecognised by economists as well as by sociologists. It covers a wide range, including child care, gardening, catering, and building. If it were not done in the domestic economy, most of it would either have to be done by paid employees or be provided by the state or by employers. For example, admission of an elderly person to local authority residential care can be seen as a transfer of work from the domestic to the formal economy.

The feminist movement has drawn attention to women's work in the household and how the devaluation of this work contributes to the subordination of women. Household labour is not usually costed in cash terms, but the 'Wages for Housework' campaign bases its arguments on an economic analysis of these costs.

Work in the community is done on both a casual and a systematic basis, ranging from giving surplus garden produce to a neighbour to acting as a volunteer driver for a day centre, or running the local branch of a national charity. A growth area in this kind of work, which has not been properly researched by sociologists, is schemes like the British Trust for Conservation Volunteers, or Community Service Volunteers, which do millions of pounds worth of work on a voluntary basis.

Much community work would otherwise have to be paid for, and it is of course the stated policy of the Thatcher government to transfer a large proportion of welfare work from the formal sector of the economy (via social work departments and social security) to the informal sector (via voluntary work and charity).

In many ways, formal and informal work are similar. 'Like work in the formal economy, work outside it is influenced by class, race and gender, by the state and by power relations and by ideologies' (Deem, 1988). Informal work has differences of status and working conditions, and it has important consequences for people's leisure, in terms of time, money, and enjoyment.

A classification scheme such as that outlined in this article is not an end in itself. Its value depends on how useful it is in helping us to analyse changes in the nature of work, particularly how economic activity is distributed between the sectors identified. In 1980, Gershuny and Pahl suggested that the increase in unemployment might mean greater activity in the household economy. But subsequent research by Pahl showed that unemployment reduced such activity, partly because it required expenditure on tools.

Similarly, if the increase in unemployment in the 1980s led to greater reliance on informal or unpaid work, or on barter, the recent reductions may see the opposite trend becoming established. More cash in people's pockets may result in their employing people to do work they previously did themselves, or left undone. Or will it rather result in a boom for the big DIY stores and garden centres?

6 MAY 1988

Discussion Topic

How might the concepts of class, race and gender be used in studying the work of Community Service Volunteers?

FURTHER READING

Deem, R. (1988) *Work, Unemployment and Leisure* (Routledge).

Gershuny, J. and Pahl, R. (1980) 'Britain in the Decade of the Three Economies', *New Society*, 3 January, 1980.

16

Football Hooliganism

What are the Causes?

Each May brings the climax of the English football season – the FA Cup Final. Until recently, the winners would automatically have qualified to play in Europe, but since the deaths resulting from crowd disorders when Liverpool played Juventus at the Heysel stadium in 1985 this has not been so.

Football hooliganism has been near the top of the agenda for both media and politicians for 20 years. Academic contributions have often taken issue with popular accounts.

Pearson (1983) refers to a match between Wolves and Chelsea when Wolves supporters attacked the Chelsea players and then 2000 of them protested about their club selling its best players. The point about these events is that they took place in 1936, a reminder that such trouble is not new. Indeed, Pearson's approach challenges the tendency to see the youth problem as new and to contrast it with a golden age, often dated to 20 years before. He traces such mistaken nostalgia back to the early 19th century and before.

A recurring feature that he notes is the way that British newspapers and politicians often blame 'alien influences', such as Hollywood films, 'continental' fouls, and immigrants (Irish or West Indian). Ironically, football hooliganism is often seen from abroad as the 'English disease', and it has recently been linked with assertions of English nationalism and racism.

Pearson's scepticism about media images is echoed by the findings of Marsh *et al.* (1978). After research at Oxford United, they argued that much of what is labelled 'mindless violence' is neither mindless nor necessarily violent. There are, they say, rules of disorder which channel the aggression. For example, boots often seem to miss their targets intentionally.

Much aggro is best understood as a way in which aggression, seen as

a natural, permanent and sometimes positive feature of human existence, is ritually expressed. Indeed, the theatre of chants, scarves and so
on may be seen as functional for, without the rules of disorder, more
real violence might take place. The Oxford fans themselves used the
term 'nutter' for those who went beyond the bounds of what they saw
as acceptable behaviour.

In contrast to the foregoing, radical criminologists have recently
argued that there has been too great a tendency to view the crime
problem as the product of media labels and police overreaction. Feminists have pointed to the way that masculinity sometimes celebrates
aggression and violence, and certainly most football hooligans are male.
Jock Young reinforces this view and refers also to the racial attacks and
abuse that members of ethnic minorities, both players and spectators,
regularly experience.

Williams *et al.* (1984) also criticise Marsh for not taking football
violence seriously enough. Their account stresses how football violence
is found particularly among the rough working class, where boys are
more frequently socialised in age- and gender-specific street cultures.
Here are located the values of toughness, territoriality, anti-authority,
group loyalty and hostility to outsiders. These values are often expressed in support of their team, but team rivalries may be dropped in
favour of national loyalties when abroad, such as in Spain for the 1982
World Cup, where foreigners were the enemy.

The issue of social class is also stressed by Taylor (1982), although
he takes a wider approach, arguing that football violence has to be seen
in the context of changes in the class structure and the role of the state
in managing these changes. He points, for example, to the impact of
economic recession on the lower working class, especially its effect on
young workers and the unemployed.

Along with this, there has been the continued break-up of working-
class communities, of the extended family, and of the cultures based on
these. One response to this among young members of this class has
been aggression and violence, often linked to white racism, sometimes
typified by skinhead culture.

Taylor links these changes in class structure, and youth responses to
them, to the series of moral panics about alleged lawlessness in the
1970s and 1980s. These moral panics enabled the capitalist state to
justify a move towards more coercive policing and government. The
social consensus of the affluent 1950s and 1960s had gone, and the
state played a more authoritarian role in keeping people in their places
– hence the growth of ideologies of law and order.

This account of sociological approaches to football hooliganism inevitably omits some issues, but one recent trend deserves particular
comment. The news media, obviously well briefed by the police, have
reported a series of highly organised undercover police operations

against apparently equally highly organised gangs of alleged football hooligans.

These operations, usually culminating in well-photographed mass arrests of alleged hooligans in their homes, together with the confiscation of quantities of weapons, are followed by highly publicised trials and sentencing. It is not clear whether this reveals the appearance of a new type of 'football hooligan', or the uncovering of something that has existed for some time.

Certainly, press reports suggest a refinement of the now familiar portrait of the football hooligan as folk devil. Dunning *et al.* refer to the rise of the organised hooligan, travelling to matches independently of special trains with their scarves and other paraphernalia, and suggest that the publicity and glamour given to lower working-class hooliganism might attract some disaffected youth from other sectors of the working class or middle class, although such involvement is likely to be only temporary.

Some media reports talk of salaried hooligans keeping press cuttings about their exploits, but this is clearly an area where more research is needed before valid analysis can be done.

13 MAY 1988

Discussion Topic

The ban on English clubs playing in Europe continues. In the light of this article, consider why this is so.

FURTHER READING

Marsh, P. *et al.* (1978) *The Rules of Disorder* (RKP).

Pearson, G. (1983) *Hooligan* (Macmillan).

Taylor, I. (1982) *'On the Soccer Violence Question'*, in D. Hargreaves *Sport, Culture and Ideology* (RKP)

Williams, J. *et al.* (1984) *Hooligans Abroad* (RKP).

17

Looking at the Evidence

Sociology and Social Policy

A rather optimistic social scientist might see the creation of the Broadcasting Standards Commission as an opportunity to exercise influence over government policy in an area of great everyday significance. After all, if such a body were appointed to oversee, say, standards of public health in the inner city, it would be reasonable to expect it to take careful note of the research findings of experts in the field. In addition, it might ask the experts to do original research into areas about which little was currently known.

Of the new commission's duties, the one that has attracted most public attention is its responsibility to monitor the amount of sex and violence on television, to preview imported material, and to advise on whether it should be shown. The underlying assumption of this is not only that such material may be offensive to some viewers, but that its appearance on television in recent years has contributed to the rising levels of recorded criminal violence. If this causal link exists, then it is logical to expect that the reduction or elimination of such material will result in a reduction in the amount of criminal violence. This remains an hypothesis, however, until sound research confirms or refutes it. In a matter of such public importance, and one that encroaches so far into the areas of censorship and civil liberty, it might be hoped that decisions would be based on social scientific evidence rather than on popular assumptions.

The first reported statements of Sir William Rees-Mogg, chairman of the new commission, suggest that this rational scientific approach is not going to be followed. It appears that, for the commission, the causal link is taken for granted, and the key issue is whether the broadcasting companies will voluntarily cooperate with the commission's activities. But, as was shown in a Society Today article (See Article 5), the link between TV violence and actual violence is far from established, though neither has it been refuted. The social scientific case is best described as non-proven. Nevertheless, the commission will proceed.

The history of the relationship between social research and social policy is uneven. An example of positive influence is in the area of educational reform in the 1950s and 1960s. As Kogan (1971) makes clear, social scientists in general, and sociologists in particular, were key figures in the educational establishment that advised politicians of both major parties, in opposition as well as in government. These advisers included people like Jean Floud, A.H. Halsey, Michael Young and David Donnison. Anthony Crosland, while Secretary of State for Education, used to hold informal gatherings of social scientists at his home. Those attending advised him on such policy matters as the introduction of comprehensive schools in the 1960s, and on the reform of higher education, with the introduction of the polytechnics.

At the root of many of these reforms lay the economists' argument that spending on education is investment as well as consumption, and the sociologists' challenge to pre-war educational psychology about the extent to which ability could be reliably predicted, and how far the predictive tests in use, mainly the eleven-plus examination, favoured children from particular social backgrounds. 'It wasn't the Department (of Education) that cracked the eleven-plus doctrine', said Crosland, 'but it was mainly such outsiders as Vaizey, Floud, Halsey, and the rest'.

In contrast to this, governmental response to the Black Report of 1980 could hardly have been more muted. The Working Group on Inequalities in Health was established in 1977, under the chairmanship of Sir Douglas Black, later to become President of the Royal College of Physicians. One of the three other members of the Group was Peter Townsend and its researcher was Nicky Hart, both from the Sociology Department at Essex University. The Report's main finding would not have been welcome to any government at that time: 'despite more than 30 years of an NHS expressly committed to offering equal care for all, there remains a marked class gradient in standards of health.'

The Report was submitted to the Secretary of State in April 1980, and, in the normal way, would have been published by the DHSS or HMSO. In this case, however, it was arranged for 260 duplicated copies of the typescript to be made publicly available in the week of August Bank Holiday 1980. This apparent attempt at concealment backfired, since the medical press were so angered by it that, in the end, the Report received more attention than it might otherwise have done, and a modified version was finally published as a paperback book in 1982.

The Secretary of State was unmoved by the furore, and questioned the Report's findings while wholly rejecting its recommendations:

'Additional expenditure on the scale which could result from the Report's recommendations (the amount involved could be upwards of two billion pounds per year) is quite unrealistic in present or any future economic circumstances, quite apart from any judgement that may be formed of the effectiveness of such expenditure in dealing with the problems identified.'

There are other areas where sociologists can claim to have had some influence, even if sometimes indirectly. The passing of Equal Opportunities legislation in the 1970s owed much to the evidence of discrimination against women and ethnic minorities that had been assembled by sociologists. In addition, sociological insights have led to changes in the training of doctors, and of the police, both in their initial training and in in-service courses, especially in the field of race relations.

Neither the theoretical nor the practical links between social research and social policy can ever be as clear-cut as can sometimes be the links between, say, biological research and the practice of medicine. Nevertheless, it could be argued that Rees-Mogg's apparent unwillingness publicly to refer to the importance of research findings to his commission's activities indicates that its creation has as much to do with catching the political moment as with the making of rational social policy.

10 JUNE 1988

Discussion Topic

How might sociological research be helpful in the training of the police and/or doctors?

FURTHER READING

Kogan, M. (1971) *The Politics of Education* (Penguin).

Townsend, P. and Davidson, N. (1982) *Inequalities in Health* (Pelican).

18

The Breeding of Abuse

Power and Dependency in Institutions

Revelations about cruel or neglectful treatment of the elderly in a tiny minority of residential homes, in both the public and the private sector, continue to be made with depressing regularity. Typically, the media's response is to seek out individuals to blame for these abuses, and to personalise what has happened in strongly-worded attacks on the activities of named persons.

The news media usually do this in an attempt to make their stories more attractive to the audience, but ordinary people's response to this kind of story tends also to emphasise the individual and to ignore the importance of the setting in which such things happen. By contrast, sociologists, in seeking to explain behaviour, will study the context and the actors in that context. Where an outside observer might ask: 'What kind of person could behave in that way towards helpless old people?', a sociologist would ask 'What kinds of social settings generate that kind of response in the people in them?'

Where the first view would see the solution to malpractice to be throwing out the rotten apples from the barrel, the second sees the barrel and the way its contents are organised as being at least as important.

Howard Becker, in an interview recorded in 1970, points out that Erving Goffman (1961), while by no means the first writer to describe what went on in mental institutions, was the first to make it clear that the abuses were:

'Not some kind of aberration . . . but rather a characteristic feature of the system. He described what were thought to be the abuses of the mental health institutions not as the work of some bad people but as the way those organisations worked, as integral features of them. Ethnographic research leads you to see that what might be thought of as pathologies are in fact integral to the systems they exist in.'

Goffman's book is usually cited with reference to the problems of institutionalisation of inmates, but the original work has just as much to say about the effects of institutional life on staff.

Experimental research also has looked at the effects on people of being placed in positions of power in institutions. Haney, Banks and Zimbardo (1973) set up a simulated prison and assigned 24 volunteers to the roles of guard and of prisoner. The 'guards' were led to believe that the focus of the research was on the behaviour of the 'prisoners'. The regulations of the 'prison' were explained, and the guards were then given the authority to run the prison within these rules.

The experiment had, however, to be ended after only six days because of the reaction of both guards and prisoners. Some prisoners were retreating into apathy by the second day, and some had to be released early because of emotional stress. Many of the guards showed enjoyment of the power they had been given and abused it, mainly through insulting the prisoners, and by transforming their rights into privileges – then arbitrarily withholding them.

The prisoners welcomed the early end of the experiment, but the guards were reluctant to give up the extreme power and control which they had exercised. There were individual differences in the behaviour of the guards, ranging from the relatively passive, through the 'tough but fair', to those who engaged in 'creative cruelty and harassment'. But no guard ever challenged the behaviour of another guard, which meant that the behaviour of the toughest guard became the norm for that shift.

There is always a question-mark over the validity of experimental evidence like this. How far is what happens in the experimental situation true of what happens in the real world? Haney *et al.* recognise this but suggest that, if these extreme reactions occur in less than a week in a situation which everyone knows to be experimental and temporary, there is an even greater probability that they will occur in a real prison.

Two key concepts are relevant to both the simulated prison and residential homes for the elderly: power and dependency. Power is an aspect of all relations of interdependence, but unequal amounts of dependency create unequal distribution of power. In the prison, the rules enabled the guards to establish a 'network of dependency relations' which 'not only promoted helplessness among the prisoners, but served to emasculate them as well'.

In homes for the elderly, the residents are by definition dependent to some extent, so the balance of dependency between residents and staff is very unequal; so, therefore, is the balance of power. To varying degrees, residents depend on staff for their physical needs, and this is likely to increase with the passing of time. In addition, while residents can upset staff from time to time, staff can undermine the residents' sense of security and emotional stability much more easily and more profoundly, even without any intention to do so.

In the final analysis, while the care staff can detach themselves when they go home, or even walk out of the job, most residents do not have this choice. This imbalance creates the risk not only of what Goffman called 'situational withdrawal' by residents, but of the routine exercise by care staff of a degree of power which easily crosses the line into cruelty, as the norms of interpersonal relations in the outside world become remote and apparently irrelevant.

Max Weber defined power as 'the probability that one actor within a social relationship will be in a position to carry out his will despite resistance, regardless of the basis on which this probability rests'. Where the parties to a relationship have roughly equal control over each other's needs and wants, each will be constrained in what they can do to the other. Where such control is markedly unequal, such constraints may disappear altogether. This is a risk of which all those who work in residential homes must be aware.

17 JUNE 1988

Discussion Topic

In what other social relationships does an imbalance of dependency create an imbalance of power? What is the outcome?

FURTHER READING

Goffman, E. (1961) *Asylums* (Doubleday; Pelican, 1968).

Haney, C., Banks, C. and Zimbardo, P. (1973) *A Study of Prisoners and Guards in a Simulated Prison.* Reprinted in D. Potter, *Society and the Social Sciences* (RKP, 1981).

19

The Sociology of Health

Epidemiology; the Work of McKeown

From time to time, a single individual makes such a telling challenge to the common-sense view of some aspect of social life that anyone who reads their work has their understanding transformed. Thomas McKeown, who died on 13 June 1988 made such a contribution. Trained as a physiologist, he was the first holder of the chair of social medicine at Birmingham University, and an international figure in the science of epidemiology.

Epidemiology is the study of how diseases are distributed within and between populations. It shows how particular conditions are not randomly distributed, but rather can be shown to vary systematically in relation to such factors as class, occupation, gender, ethnicity, and region. The sociology of health takes this data further. Mainstream epidemiology retains the medical model of disease, which emphasises the related notions of the body as a machine and the treatment and cure of diseased individuals as occurring in isolation from their social environment. Sociologists direct attention to the importance of the social context and social relationships as causes of and not just variables in people's varying experience of health and ill-health. It is on this area that McKeown focused and to which he brought fresh insights.

Most people know that in Britain today compared with the early 19th century, life expectancy at birth is longer, child mortality has fallen dramatically, and there has been a substantial increase in population. The common-sense view is that modern medicine can take the credit for these changes, having identified the causes of the major killer diseases. These discoveries, it is assumed, have enabled us to prevent or cure them. Indeed, much of the status of modern medicine rests on this belief. McKeown set out to examine this view, basing his argument on detailed analysis of mortality and morbidity (illness) statistics from the 19th century to the present, and relating these to medical developments over the same period.

The rapid increase in population was caused in its early stages by a declining death rate, especially among young children. This decline in mortality, which started in about 1830, had several causes, but about 60 per cent of it was due to a reduction in the incidence and fatal effect of the major epidemic diseases, including typhoid, cholera, tuberculosis, scarlet fever, whooping cough and measles, which are transmitted through water, through food, and through the air. McKeown examined a number of factors, including medical progress, which might have contributed to the reduction in the impact of these diseases, and settled on three as being the most important: public hygiene (clean water supplies, effective waste disposal, better housing); contraception (which meant that fewer women died in or after childbirth, and that babies received more attention); and nutrition (a better diet, and more of it). Of these, improved nutritional standards, arising from increased production of food, are the most important, since they result in people having greater resistance to infections. Significantly, the same pattern is seen in the Third World today. Many children, particularly, die of diet-related conditions, if not of simple starvation, but many more die of diseases such as measles and diarrhoea. They just do not have the resistance that makes these diseases little more than temporary inconvenience in richer countries.

The key point that McKeown made was that most of the improvements in health and life expectancy in Britain took place *before* the 1930s, whereas most of the great breakthroughs of modern curative medicine, like the sulphonamides, antibiotics, vaccinations and so on have been introduced *since* that date. They have contributed to improved health, of course, especially between the 1930s and the 1950s, but only on a minor scale in historical terms. For McKeown the key factors in improving health have been social and environmental, not medical.

In questioning the common-sense view of the relationship between health and medicine, McKeown's work challenges the ideology that underpins the power of the medical profession. Indeed, it is the fact that this ideology has been accepted as common-sense that gives it its strength. McKeown's analysis (which has not gone unchallenged either within or outside sociology), by relegating curative, hospital-oriented and technological medicine to a minor role in terms of its contribution to improved health standards, undermines the status and power of the orthodox medical professions. He argues that the resources being allocated to medical services, especially to hospitals, are misdirected, because they are based on mistaken ideas about the basis of health. Modern medicine has resulted in 'indifference to the external influence and personal behaviour which are the predominant determinants of health'. (McKeown, 1976).

The work of McKeown and others lies behind the growing belief, in official and lay circles, that there are more effective ways of promoting good health than by expensive technological 'breakthroughs'. In the poorer countries, this has resulted in the use of simple universal measures rather than investment in expensive hospitals, and in the richer countries in campaigns against smoking, for healthy eating and more exercise, 'safe sex' and so on. There is, however, some difference in emphasis between the campaigns publicised by the junior health minister, Mrs Edwina Currie, and McKeown's analysis. Mrs Currie's campaigns, in line with government philosophy, emphasise the individual's responsibility for their own health, through taking exercise, eating a balanced diet, and not smoking. McKeown would of course accept these as a necessary element in preventive medicine, but would stress that some measures, such as the control of pollution, the improvement of working conditions, the urban environment, and better housing, are outside the control of the individual and should be the responsibility of the state. He says: 'Past improvement has been due mainly to modification of behaviour and changes in the environment, and it is to these same influences that we must look particularly for further advance'.

8 JULY 1988

Discussion Topic

Why does the state concern itself with the health of its citizens? How far should it do so?

FURTHER READING

McKeown, T. (1976) *The Modern Rise of Population* (Edward Arnold).
McKeown, T. (1980) *The Role of Medicine* (NPHT).
Tuckett, D. (1976) *An Introduction to Medical Sociology* (Tavistock).

20

The Rules of Social Life

Understanding Everyday Action

The students for whom these articles are written enjoy long summer holidays and most will put their studies of sociology on one side during that time. That's fair enough, but it is no reason to stop studying and observing social life, and the holiday period provides many opportunities for this. Holidays are a time when the unwritten rules and conventions of everyday life are widely breached, and other rules, recognisably those of 'being-on-holiday', come into force.

Take clothing, for example. The middle-aged man dressed in shorts, sandals and a patterned shirt, open at the neck, with a straw hat on his head, is scarcely recognisable as the sober-suited professional commuter who travels into the office for the rest of the year. By wearing these clothes, he is telling the world, and himself, that he is on holiday, that many of his usual social obligations are suspended, and that he can behave in ways that he would not contemplate in the work setting, and which he assumes will not be witnessed by colleagues. An unwritten rule of holiday-making (and of works outings and office parties) is that indiscretions and excesses are not held against you in the work situation. Our man's children also know that he is operating with different rules from those of everyday life, especially those concerned with what counts as a waste of money.

Walking along a busy pavement is something we do almost every day of our lives, and we do it pretty well. That is, we get where we want to go, without bumping into people on the way, and without giving offence to other pedestrians. If we think about this at all, we think we are doing it 'automatically', and in a sense we are. But we had once to learn how to do it, and we are working at it and obeying the rules all the time, though at a level where we only become aware of it when a problem arises.

Imagine that you are walking along a narrow pavement, on your own, when you see two people coming towards you from the opposite direction. How do you pass them? A basic rule is that you do not pass between two people who are walking 'together'. But how do you recognise that they are together? If they are holding hands, there is no problem. But if not, how close do they have to be to each other before it becomes rude or aggressive to walk between them? How do the ages and the genders of the three of you affect the rules? What if they are both members of the police force? What if you are? Can they be further apart and yet still be together?

Another situation: you are walking along a deserted street after midnight, on your way home after a late party. Someone appears from a side street on your side of the road and twenty yards ahead, and turns along the pavement on which you are walking, and in the same direction. You find that you are walking along behind them, but slightly faster, so you are catching them up. You do not want them to think they are being followed, so what do you do? Walk more quietly? More noisily? Start whistling? Slow down? Speed up? Carry on at the same speed, but break into a trot a few yards before you reach them, continuing until you are safely past, perhaps with a muttered 'good night' as you go by? Or do you cross the road and overtake on that side? How would your actions vary with the age and sex of the other person? What if there were two of them?

Now imagine that you are the person in front, and you have just become aware of the person behind you. Which action by them would you find most reassuring? And which would you find most worrying?

The example of how strangers, arriving one at a time, sit on a park bench is well known, but less well documented are the niceties of etiquette that are observable in men's public lavatories as each new arrival has to decide which stall to use. If there is a row of stalls, and only one other user, it is not appropriate to make use of the immediately neighbouring one, but it is perhaps overdoing it a bit to go as far away as possible. How is the choice made? What is the etiquette in the ladies'?

Shoplifting is governed by deeply subtle rules. The serious shoplifter strives to give the impression of being in the shop simply to look and perhaps to buy, and takes great care to conceal that they are shoplifting. This is largely a negative activity, avoiding actions which will arouse suspicion. But people who are not shoplifting sometimes become aware that their browsing could look suspicious, so they conspicuously do 'not shoplifting'. This is not just the negative activity of 'not shoplifting', but the positive activity of 'doing not-shoplifting'. It might involve holding the hands and arms in awkward positions, or ostentatiously waving items in the air as you walk round the shop. Watching someone in this situation is particularly interesting because they are usually unsure whether they have an audience, so they do not know which way to direct their performance. It is possible to provoke 'doing not-shop-lifting' by doing 'being a store-detective'.

Girls and women have to learn how to do waiting-for-a-friend-in-a-public-place, and how this differs from doing waiting-to-be-picked-up. The former usually involves a girl conspicuously looking in shop windows, at her watch, and up and down the street, but carefully avoiding eye-contact with any male stranger. Men have to learn how to recognise these signals, and to distinguish them from those of the girl who is looking for a customer or a casual pick-up. The rules for the prostitute are largely the obverse of those used by the girl with an appointment.

All such rules are both produced and recognised by social actors, and they exist only as long as they are continually so produced and recognised. But, of course, mistakes can occur in both production and recognition. Most commonly, these mistakes are made by children, who have not yet learned the rules, and by people who find themselves in unfamiliar settings, such as on foreign holidays. Many social *faux pas* are simply a matter of not knowing what the rules are, and so failing to observe them or failing to recognise them. Most people protect themselves in these situations by 'keeping their head down' until they feel they have a grasp of the situation they are in. In doing this, they are in effect conducting a small-scale piece of social research. Many more rules can, however, be identified through systematic and conscious observation, and is a good way to while away those idle holiday hours.

15 JULY 1988

Discussion Topic

What are the rules for travelling on an underground train?

21

Sport and Leisure

The Role of Sport in Society

Given the feast, or perhaps surfeit, of televised sport that is available on all the TV channels it is a pity that the sociology of sport does not feature in A-level syllabuses. There is no shortage of sociological literature about sport, both descriptive and analytic, but at A-level it is, at best, just a part of the sociology of leisure.

Leisure can be thought of as a state of being or an attitude of mind which occurs in time that is left over after necessary life-tasks have been completed. It is a qualitative state. This quality is linked with the notion of play, which is activity undertaken, often spontaneously, for its intrinsic pleasure. Play activity is associated with recreation, but recreation is more routinised and may be undertaken for reasons additional to those of personal enjoyment. Sport is a form of recreation, involving physical activities similar to those of play, but with some sort of administrative arrangements, a set of agreed rules and, usually, some elements of competition or challenge with a definite outcome, often in terms of winners and losers defined primarily in respect of physical skills.

Such conceptual distinctions are not easily applied in the real world. For example, the same physical activity can fall into different categories on different occasions. Thus angling, mainly a recreational activity, becomes a sport when it is competitive. Similarly, jogging is recreation whose sporting equivalent is track, cross-country or road-racing. But what then of the London Marathon? It is competitive sport for some participants, but is recreation, albeit strenuous recreation, for others. Darts is a sport when played in competition for money, but for the great majority of players it is recreation.

Most sociological theorising about sport has been from a structural standpoint and has considered the role in society of both spectator sport and participant sport. George Mead saw the function of participatory sport as being primarily that of socialisation, through which children learn about role-taking and following rules and so about participating in social life. Taking part in organised sporting activity is like participating in a miniature social world. For adults, taking part in sport may offer an escape from work, but at the same time reinforces the value of effort, work and competitiveness.

Watching sport can provide a sense of identity and of group loyalty and may provide an outlet for aggression. Ideally such an outlet diverts aggression from other targets, though recent research into violence among spectators, not only in the context of football, suggests that this may not be the case. Watching professional wrestling, on the other hand, is very obviously cathartic for many members of the audience. Wrestling provides a good example of another value promoted by sport, that good guys win. In professional wrestling the 'goodie' beats the 'baddie', exemplifying the triumph of social justice over injustice.

The functionalist notion of the reinforcing of central norms and values has its counterpart in the Marxist notion of the reinforcement of dominant ideology. This argues that modern sport operates as a means of social control, especially in the context of school sport, promoting the ethic of hard work, competitiveness and deferred gratification. Sport is work in another guise. The apparent equality of opportunity in sport is as much of a sham as it is in the wider society, where, it is argued, the powerful and the privileged have better facilities to develop their talents, while enough 'rags-to-riches' stories exist to maintain the myth. Where once sports like football and boxing gave opportunities to a few individuals from the urban working class and from economically deprived areas of the country, they now provide avenues of upward mobility for the new proletariat, Britain's black population. A radical perspective also emphasises the profit element in modern organised sport and the huge and growing commercialism of all sport. Since commercial success depends on attracting spectators and promoting brand loyalties for sports equipment, modern spectator sport is firmly established, via TV, as mass entertainment.

Nowhere are these developments more apparent than in the Olympic Games, which has a higher spectator/participant ratio than any other sporting event. An event which was founded in its modern form at the end of the last century to celebrate the ideals of the gifted amateur and of international co-operation is now conspicuous, at least in its media presentation, for its domination by full-time athletes and its rampant nationalism, exemplified by the flag-waving of the opening ceremony and by the playing of national anthems when medals are presented.

Sexism is also a dominant theme of the Games, where only a few events, such as show-jumping, involve men and women competing together and on equal terms, though others like shooting, have no obviously built-in physical advantages for men. It could be argued that the basis of male superiority in sport is biological and hence inevitable. A more subtle analysis suggests that it is those areas of physical activity in which men excel biologically that are identified as the important sports, and that this is itself the result of male domination of such choices.

Race and ethnicity too are important aspects of the Games with certain events, such as swimming, being dominated by white athletes, while many medals for track athletics will be won by black runners. Similarly, the wealthy countries of the world lead the medal tables at the end of the Games, the result of their ability to devote large amounts of their economic surplus to sports facilities and training resources for well-nourished athletes.

The contradiction of the Games is that they are presented as the ideal of international co-operation and peace, but in practice celebrate individualism, competitiveness and nationalism.

16 SEPTEMBER 1988

Discussion Topic

Compare the media presentation of pop stars with that of top athletes.

FURTHER READING

Hargreaves, J. (1982) *Sport, Culture and Ideology* (Routledge & Kegan Paul).

22

The Changing Generation Gap

| *Understanding Age-groups* |

There has been much talk in the last ten years of a 'lost generation' of young people, of hundreds of thousands being thrown on the scrap-heap of unemployment, and of the despair and rejection that is experienced by the victims. Students today, however, find themselves in a very different situation, with advertisements in the press reminding employers that young trainees are about to become a scarce resource, and higher education institutions recognising that they must recruit a larger proportion of the age-group if they are to maintain their intake.

Almost overnight, it seems, the young have become a scarce and desirable commodity. But no one should be surprised by this. Demographers, who study the changing size, composition and distribution of human populations, recorded the steady decrease in the number of births from the late 1960s, and schools have felt the results of this in the last ten years, as the smaller age-groups have worked through the system.

At its simplest, age is a matter of how much time has passed since an individual was born, and age-groups are groups of people born within a particular period of years. Societies vary widely in the social and cultural meaning which they attach to these categories and, in a fast-changing society such as ours, successive age-groups may have very different life experiences. But it is easy to over-generalise about the experience of a particular age-group, and sociologists have been as guilty of this as anyone else, especially when discussing the younger generation.

Some generalisations are more sound than others, of course. There is some truth, for example, in the observation that people who were of an age to be on active service in the last war may find it hard to come to terms with the views of their juniors when issues of national loyalty and patriotism are discussed. It is likely that the very elderly today, brought up before the Great War, will have a more deferential attitude towards their 'betters' than young people.

But there is a near-mythology of the 1960s as a period when all young people rejected traditional values and authority structures and inaugurated what Roszak called a counter-culture. It is true that many young people at that time, especially in the United States, were profoundly affected by the controversy about the war in Vietnam and by the discovery that it was possible to influence political decision-making through mass activism. Contemporary legislation on abortion, homosexuality, divorce, and so on demonstrated that there was support for changing attitudes towards moral values and individual civil rights.

Despite widespread pessimism about the likelihood of nuclear holocaust, there was also optimism about personal opportunity and that the world could be improved by rejecting materialist values. But it is misleading to suggest that all young people in the 1960s shared in this experience in the same way or were all part of the counter-culture, any more than it is true to say that everyone in their forties is a superannuated hippy.

To help avoid such crude stereotyping, we can look to Karl Mannheim's (1952) refinement of the concept of generation. He distinguished between generation as Location (the simple age-group) and generation as Actuality, which emphasises the importance of the collective social and political experience of age-groups, leading to a shared consciousness and world-view that is unique to that group. In a changing society, this means that there will be differences and possibly conflicts between the world-views of different age-groups.

But Mannheim was careful also to develop the concept of a generational unit, which draws attention to the fact that sub-groups within a generation experience the world and its contradictions in different ways, structured by such variables as class, gender, ethnic background, and even region of residence. Thus, though it is statistically the case that youth unemployment rose to record levels in the early eighties, this did not result in all young people feeling rejected and alienated. The experience of the statistical fact was different in northern and southern Britain, in urban and rural communities, for females and males, and for members of different social classes. In the more prosperous towns of the Home Counties only the very poorly qualified were unable to find any work at all, though this was relatively commonplace among the well-qualified in some areas further north and west.

The concept of the generational unit makes it easier to consider conflict within as well as between generations, and thus to develop a more valid picture of a variety of youth sub-cultures, rather than an over-simplified and monolithic portrayal of youth as a single group, all with the same shared experience and hence the same world-view. Similarly, increasing demand for young workers and for students will not affect all generational units in the same way, though the nineties generation may have more in common with that of the sixties than is apparent at first sight. Though their values may be different, they will have in common the experience of being in demand by employers and by colleges, and perhaps of the sense that the world is a place of opportunity rather than of rejection.

The young will not be alone in this experience, for theirs is not the only generation which will be affected by the demographic changes. As employers find themselves unable to find enough young recruits, they will have to attract the middle-aged, especially women, back to work, and will have to offer pay, hours and working conditions that make it worthwhile to return. No more of the 'if you don't like the job, there's plenty more in the queue'.

Rather than being rejected as not worth training, older workers may find retraining schemes being developed for them. Already higher education institutions, aware of the fall in the number of 18-year-olds, are discovering the potential of mature students as undergraduates, and are modifying their entry requirements to enable them to qualify for entry on equal terms. But, just as it is a mistake to generalise about the young, so the middle-aged generation includes units whose experience of these changes will be mediated by their gender, colour and class. It will still be an advantage to be male, white, and to live near London.

23 SEPTEMBER 1988

Discussion Topic

Falling school rolls, and a shortage of young workers: what will be the future effects of this reduced age-group?

FURTHER READING

Mannheim, K. (1952) *Essays on the Sociology of Knowledge* (RKP).
O'Donnell, M. (1985) *Age and Generation* (Tavistock).

23

Forever on the Move

The Sociology of Migration

In a very low-key announcement in September 1988, the Home Office released statistics showing that immigration to Britain rose in the past year, ending a ten-year trend of steady decline. Admissions in the year to June 1988 were 46,600 compared with 45,300 in the previous year. The increase was the expected result of minor changes in the regulations.

An extra 46,600 into a country with a population of 55 million? Adding 0.08 per cent to the population? Hardly a matter of Britain being swamped by outsiders. In the last 30 years, however, discussion of migration in this country has been bedevilled by myth, confusion and misapprehension, often fuelled by racism. More attention has been paid to immigration than to emigration, and far more to New Commonwealth immigrants than others.

The central myth about migration rests on the idea that it is normal for human beings to stay in one place, and that societies are essentially static and self-contained. But the observer from an orbiting spacecraft, at any period in history, would have seen a very different picture: nomadic peoples following their herds or gathering food from the areas they move through; medieval caravans moving through Asia and Africa; millions of Africans being taken to the Americas as slaves in the 18th century; the exporting of millions of people from Europe to the colonies in the 19th century; the westward drive of white settlers across North America and the retreat of the Indian tribes; millions leaving Ireland in the second half of the century.

Today the observer would see commuters travelling within and between countries, holiday-makers and tourists, migrant workers, armies, and refugees.

Not all of these movements can properly be called migration, which has a spatial, a temporal and a social dimension. It involves significant movement (rather than just moving house in the same area), for a sustained period of time (rather than just for a holiday) and with major consequences for the social status and relationships of the migrant. The reasons for such migration are many and complex, but most people on the move are looking to improve their living standards or their safety.

Leaving aside migrations that are the result of war, disaster or famine, the most common reason for people moving from one place or country to another in the modern world is the search for work. One sort of explanation for this rests on the classical *laissez-faire* economic model of man as a rational being, making choices to maximise his material well-being. People do, of course, often act to better themselves, but this picture tends to assume that the person making the choice has a perfect knowledge of all the alternatives, and that the benefits sought are entirely material. It emphasises the motivation of the individual actor and neglects the fact that the choices people can make are severely constrained by factors beyond their control.

In fact the opportunities available to any particular person and their response to those opportunities are the product of social structure. An individual's decision about migration will be shaped by their perception of what migration is about, and by their sense of ties to place, or obligations to family. In addition, even if people do choose to emigrate, their ability to act on this decision will be affected by their social and financial obligations, their knowledge of possibilities, legislation in force at the time, and whether their skills match those required in the receiving country. The desire or willingness to migrate does not automatically mean the opportunity to do so.

A contrasting model of patterns of labour migration stresses that they reflect the worldwide division of labour, and the distribution of the world's wealth. Petras has argued that the world economy can be described in terms of a core of wealthy countries, such as Europe and America, a semi-periphery of the less prosperous, and a periphery of the poorest countries. The core dominates the periphery, which provides a pool of reserve labour for the core countries, which call upon this reserve when it suits them to do so, but restrict immigration when the home labour market is adequately supplied.

There is a dual labour market within each core country, whereby well-paid, secure and skilled jobs are filled internally, leaving unskilled jobs to be filled by migrant labour. The main West Indian and Asian immigration to the UK in the 1950s and the 1960s fits this pattern, as the demand for labour, especially in low-paid, low status work in the public sector, outstripped the supply.

The same pattern can be seen today in South America, between Mexico and the United States, and in Europe. Turkey supplies labour to Germany and Sweden, Spain and Portugal to France and Germany, North Africa to France, and Ireland to England. The pattern also exists in South Africa, and within the UK, with labour movement from Wales and Scotland to England, and from north and west England to the south.

It is important to recognise, though, that many of these people are more properly seen as migrant workers (or, in the German expression, 'guest-workers') than as settlers, for they leave their families at home and remit money back, returning when they can afford to or, more usually, when the host country decides it has no further use for them. The disruption to family and community life in the country supplying the labour, as well as the effect of the loss of a key section of its own labour-force, is considerable.

The first of these models, then, emphasises the motivation and decision of the migrant seen as a free agent, and so is in tune with an action perspective in sociological theory. It asks no questions about why some areas offer better prospects than others. The second model draws on the sociology of development and emphasises external factors shaping the labour market. It is therefore a structural perspective, portraying individual actors as more constrained in their choices. There is more to migration than simply getting on your bike.

7 OCTOBER 1988

Discussion Topic

Identify and discuss the factors that would influence you if you were thinking about emigrating.

FURTHER READING

Jackson, J.A. (1986) *Migration* (Longman).

24

Handicapping the Disabled

The Consequences of Labelling

The Minister for the Disabled was embarrassed on 28 September 1988 by the Office of Population Censuses and Surveys. It published a report which suggested that there are 6.2 million disabled adults in Britain today, twice as many as previous estimates which were based on a survey carried out in 1969. The new figures are politically embarrassing because of the implications for public spending if the needs of this group are to be met. Peter Townsend, in *Poverty in the United Kingdom* (1979) had already suggested that the official estimate was about half the correct figure, but his estimate was rubbished on the grounds that his definitions, both of poverty and of disability, were too generous.

This is the nub of the matter. The OPCS, guided by the Department of Health, set a relatively low threshold for disability. The minister pointed out that two million people are in the lowest two of the ten categories and argued that many of those included would not regard themselves as disabled. He said that older people (4.3 of the 6.2 million are over 60), 'would consider the relatively minor limitations of hearing, vision or movement recorded by the survey as in fact normal for their age'.

With this comment, the minister entered a terminological minefield, in which the concepts of normal, impairment, disability and handicap are found. The latter three terms are often used interchangeably, but the World Health Organisation, and British law, tries to clarify the difference between their meanings. Impairment refers to having any limb, organ or mechanism of the body that is defective or missing. For example, many people's eyesight is impaired. Disability refers to the lack of function that results directly from the impairment, (some people cannot see distant objects clearly). Handicap refers to the limitations on normal activity that result from the disability (in the case of short sight, then, there may be little handicap in everyday life, and none if spectacles are worn).

In the 1981 Year of the Disabled, the emphasis was on helping disabled people to adjust, physically and psychologically, to society. Shearer, from a more sociological standpoint, turns the problem round. She emphasises that handicap, whether physical, emotional, social or a combination of these, is about the relationship between people with disabilities and their environment. Whereas impairment and disability are a matter of an individual's condition, handicap is often imposed on a disability by the environment, making it more limiting than it need necessarily be. Thus, the loss of both legs is an impairment and disabling for mobility, but the physical handicap is generated by a world arranged for people who can walk.

While it may be that not much can be done about impairment or disability, this may not be true of handicap. Instead of stressing how disabled people can adjust to their environment, the environment can be changed to reduce handicap. One aspect of such changes concerns practical things like installing ramps, widening doors, and improving lighting facilities. But changing attitudes is just as important, for they can be even more handicapping than physical surroundings.

The phrase 'the disabled' reflects such attitudes, for it implies that people with disabilities are fundamentally different from 'normal' people. But, as Shearer argues, 'the mix of abilities that goes to make up the human race is a broad one', ranging from people who are confined to wheelchairs to Olympic athletes, and from someone who can win a Nobel prize to someone who has difficulty in paying the right amount in shops.

Every individual is a mix of strengths and weaknesses, abilities and inabilities. Most people can organise their lives so that their strengths are maximised and their inabilities minimised. But certain disabilities result in a person being labelled 'disabled'. We do not talk of 'the fats' or 'the myopics', but we do talk of 'spastics' and 'the blind'. This becomes their master-status and their handicap. Shearer again: 'By turning a description of a condition into a description of people, we are saying that this is really all we need to know about them. We confirm their abnormality'.

What this amounts to is that people with disabilities are deviant. This may seem a cruel statement, but the quality of deviance, as Howard Becker argued, lies not in actions but in reactions. The term 'deviant' is usually reserved for people who are held to blame for their actions, like thieves, drug addicts or hooligans, and it seems inappropriate to use it to refer to elderly people or those who suffer from psychiatric illness or a physical deformity. But such people are treated in the same way as culpable deviants: they are at risk of being stigmatised, socially isolated, stereotyped and even segregated into the company of others with the same label.

They are handicapped not so much by their disability as by the social reaction to it, for their every action is interpreted in terms of their disability. For example, many people talk to themselves when they think they are alone. Sometimes they are overheard, and perhaps someone makes a joke about it. But if the person is known to have a history of psychiatric illness, the talking is likely to be interpreted as a symptom of illness, and as further evidence of the correctness of the initial label.

Labelling theory argues that we interpret the actions of others in terms of what we 'know' about them, and that our interpretations confirm our 'knowledge'. If what we 'know' is that the person is deviant, our interpretation tends to reinforce the stigmatisation of the deviant person. This is not inevitable. Davis has shown how people with visible handicaps may use one of several strategies to deny or disavow their deviance, and so resist the label.

The bureaucratic requirement for detailed definitions and information about people with disabilities, though intended to help in reducing their handicap by making better welfare provision, may in fact reinforce their greatest handicap: being set apart as a special, deviant group of people.

14 OCTOBER 1988

Discussion Topic

Is it possible to make a clear distinction between culpable and non-culpable deviance?

FURTHER READING

Shearer, A. (1981) *Disability; Whose Handicap?* (Blackwell).

Davis, F. (1961) 'Deviance Disavowal', in H. Becker, *The Other Side* (Collier-Macmillan Free Press).

25

The Battle for Common Sense

The Power of Ideology

Mrs Thatcher has been Prime Minister for more than half the life-time of anyone aged 17 years or less. This means that for the great majority of the age group she has, in effect, always been Prime Minister. Since we tend to see as normal the state of affairs into which we are socialised, it follows that the next generation of voters may find it hard to conceive of a male Prime Minister, a Labour Prime Minister, or even of one who is not Mrs Thatcher. Her pre-eminence is made the greater by her personal style of leadership, demonstrated in her performance at the Conservative Party conference each year.

There is some precedent for all this in the period from 1951 to 1964, when the Conservatives won a succession of general elections and became able to present themselves as the 'natural party of government'. However, there were several Prime Ministers in that period and none achieved the personal stature of Mrs Thatcher, and none had a set of politico-economic beliefs named after them, as in 'Thatcherism'.

The expression 'natural party of government' is significant. Describing something as 'natural' implies that it is fixed and inevitable, governed by natural laws, so that it is flying in the face of common sense to suggest that things could be otherwise than they are. Such arguments form the basis of the biological arguments sometimes used to justify domination based on race or on gender. As long as those with power can convince the powerless that things are as they are because this is the natural order of things, their position hardly needs defending, and certainly not by force.

Clearly, Mrs Thatcher's premiership and policies are not really part of the natural order of things but the more people who find it hard to imagine alternatives, the stronger her position becomes. And as the set of ideas which underpin Thatcherism, sometimes referred to by the term 'New Right', become more widely taken for granted and treated as common sense, so any challenge to them is less likely to succeed.

The concept of hegemony, which was developed in the work of Antonio Gramsci in the 1920s and 1930s, refers to 'moral and philosophical leadership, which is attained through the active consent of major groups in a society' (Bocock, 1986). Traditional Marxism stresses that political power is rooted in the economic system, and that political ideas and world-views are a reflection of this. Gramsci, by contrast, argued that successful control by a dominant class depends on its projecting its particular views so effectively that they come to be seen as natural and common sense by those who are in fact subordinated to them.

Gramsci used the term in his discussion of how groups and classes achieve political power, and how, having gained it, they hold on to it. He argued that, while it is possible to seize political power by force and to retain it by coercion, the successful exercise of power depends on achieving hegemonic domination. The mass of the people come to regard as normal, natural and unchallengeable what is, in Marx's terms, ruling class ideology. Hegemony then operates at two levels: as the common-sense view of the masses, and as a set of principles spelled out by political thinkers (intellectuals) which, in turn, form the basis and the rationale for government policy.

But just how widely is Thatcherism accepted? Is it, in any sense, hegemonic? It has certainly seen off what had come to be known as the post-war consensus on welfare. From the 1940s to the late 1970s, there appeared to be substantial agreement between the major political parties on the proper role of the state in modern society, which was to intervene to a considerable degree to modify the effects of the free market in matters of health, education, welfare and poverty.

The emergence of the New Right, in the United States as well as in Britain, has broken up this consensus. The mainstream view in post-war political life is now openly derided by senior politicians, and by much of the press, as the outdated views of a minority with suspicious affinities with socialism and other alleged enemies of democracy. We are encouraged to believe that the proper role of the state is to take a back seat in welfare matters, and to let the free market operate in matters of investment, production, consumption, employment etc, in the expectation that the anticipated benefits will, sooner or later, be felt by all.

But is this non-interventionist version of liberalism generally accepted? What evidence could be cited in answer to this question? Does the fact that Mrs Thatcher has won three consecutive elections point to her policies having achieved hegemonic domination? Or is this rather an outcome of our electoral system, where a party winning a minority of votes can win a substantial majority of parliamentary seats? Or is it the outcome of divisions and disorganisation among the opposition? In any case, there are large areas of the United Kingdom, such as Scotland, where the Tories' electoral success has been slight.

The British Attitude Survey has found that, from 1983 to 1986, support for certain basic principles of Thatcherism actually declined.

'Readiness to pay increased taxes to provide welfare services has grown substantially . . . from around a third of the population to nearly half . . . . These public attitudes run counter to the policies of the 1979 and 1983 Conservative governments which have tended to advocate tax cuts at the expense of welfare spending, private provision in place of state welfare and targeted services rather than the universal standards of social provision and care. Presumably the electoral success of the Conservatives cannot be explained by public support for their policies on welfare spending.'

Despite making major changes in the role of the state in British society, especially in welfare, it appears that Mrs Thatcher's governments have not convinced the majority of the electorate of the morality, let alone the common sense, of these policies.

21 OCTOBER 1988

Discussion Topic

How can support for government policies be reliably measured?

FURTHER READING

Bocock, R. (1986) *Hegemony* (Tavistock).
Jowell, R. (1987) *'British Social Attitudes: the 1987 Report'* (Gower).

26

Paradise Lost?

The Concept of Community

Bath, Chester, Scarborough, St Austell. What have these towns in common? Most people's response would probably be something about their all being quiet market or holiday towns. And yet in 1988 they were all included in Mr Hurd's list of towns where drinking alcohol in public has been banned, in an attempt to deal with the recent increase in loutish behaviour associated with drunkenness. The ban was a key step in the official response to one of 1988's moral panics . . . rural violence.

The first signs came early in the year when incidents of fighting between police and drunken youths began to be reported from hitherto innocuous places such as High Wycombe, Windsor and Farnham. The Chief Constables of Thames Valley and of Devon and Cornwall, among others, expressed their concern publicly, and the media reportage developed in the classic manner of a moral panic, as reports came in from more and more unlikely places. To call this response a moral panic is not to imply that the events did not take place, but to draw attention to how they have been responded to in the media and by the authorities.

Part of the key to understanding this response lies in recognising that the phrase 'rural violence' is contradictory. Where 'violence' has ugly and negative connotations, 'rural' connotes peace, harmony, quiet, and the ideal community. We can cope with the concept of 'urban riots' and 'inner-city crime' because the connotations are congruent.

This ideal, long established in literature and the arts, has its sociological roots in the concept of 'community' as this was developed in the 19th century, particularly by Ferdinand Tonnies. In his book *Gemeinschaft und Gesellschaft*, published in 1887, Tonnies contrasted two ideal types of social relationship. *Gemeinschaft* (usually translated as 'community') relationships are face-to-face, involving intimate personal contact and shared values. They are centred on religion, family and neighbourhood. Everyone is integrated into the close-knit community, in which there is a strong sense of belonging and an orderly existence.

By contrast, *Gesellschaft* (translated as 'association') relationships are more impersonal, entered into as a means to an end, governed by contracts, and with limited responsibilities. Such relationships are transitory and superficial.

While Tonnies described these as ideal types, and therefore as having no actual existence in the real world, it is clear that he associated *Gemeinschaft* with pre-industrial society, villages and rural communities, and *Gesellschaft* with industrial society and city life.

Like other sociologists of his time, Tonnies was reinforcing the idea that relationships in urban industrial societies are impersonal, self-interested, alienating, more squalid and more prone to conflict and stress than were pre-industrial societies, though the rural areas of industrial societies will retain some of the better characteristics of the past. This view has come to be known as the 'loss of community thesis'.

The work of Tonnies and others gave rise to the tradition of community studies in sociology, both in America and in Britain, wherein researchers spent a period of time as participant observers in small supposedly self-contained communities, producing ethnographic accounts of their way of life. Most of this empirical work incorporates the romantic notion of community, with researchers largely confirming the model 'rural = *gemeinschaft* = good': 'urban = *gesellschaft* = bad'.

By the 1930s, however, Tonnies' two-part model was being challenged by those who argued that communities were better seen as being ranged along a continuum from the wholly rural to the wholly urban, rather than as being one or the other. Robert Redfield, in Chicago in the 1930s, identified a folk-urban continuum, the 'folk' end being exemplified by the Mexican village of Tepoztlan, of which he made an anthropological study.

In the 1960s, this modified version was challenged in its turn. Willmott and Young, in their studies of East London, showed that *Gemeinschaft* communities flourished in the city. Class divisions were found by researchers studying small villages. Pahl, in a study of commuter villages in Hertfordshire, found some of the impersonality and conflict of the city, with villages being divided into locals and newcomers. As early as the late 1940s, Oscar Lewis revisited Tepoztlan and, using rather different research methods, found it divided by dissent and conflict.

Though these studies forced a reappraisal of the over-simplified model of two distinct types of society, they did little to break down the myth of the rural idyll. It was the historical work of writers like Raymond Williams and Peter Laslett that showed how the rural life of the past was, for the great majority of people, anything but idyllic. Williams, in *The Country and the City* (1973) argued that life in medieval villages was pretty dreadful. Close-knit it may have been, but this meant spying, prying, back-biting and conflict. Such harmony as was found among the exploited peasantry was a defence against the landlord, the 'mutuality of the oppressed'.

As a descriptive term, 'community' has been used in so many different ways that most sociologists have abandoned it in favour of terms like 'network' and 'social system'. But, as an ideal, it persists. Indeed, the word is now so value-laden that it is impossible to think of its being used in a negative way. The use of the word in situations where conflict is present or anticipated seems often to reflect an attempt to deny or conceal that the conflict is there.

The ideal of community is part and parcel of English nostalgia for the 'good old days', cottages with roses round the door, milk warm from the cow, and the elderly rustic sitting in the sun outside the pub with his pint of ale. Except that today, in Bath and Chester, he would have to take his pint indoors.

28 OCTOBER 1988

Discussion Topic

Discuss the reputations of some other towns. Are they justified?

FURTHER READING

Bell, C and Newby, H. (1971) *Community Studies* (George Allen and Unwin).

27

The Irish Gag

Censorship and the Media

When the government decided in 1988 to ban the broadcasting of interviews with, or speeches by, representatives of certain organisations involved in the Northern Ireland conflict, all they had to do was issue a directive to the BBC and the IBA.

The legal powers invoked are embodied in the BBC's charter, drawn up in 1927, and in the Broadcasting Act of 1981, which regulates the IBA and includes the statement that the Home Secretary may 'at any time require the authority to refrain from broadcasting any matter or classes of matter specified'. For some observers, such power comes uncomfortably close to political censorship, which is thought to have no place in a democratic society.

The relationship between the mass media, especially television, and the state is often described as one of interdependence. 'The media and the state – the whole apparatus of government – are in two minds about each other. On the one hand, a certain tension separates them; on the other, undeniable ties bind them' (Whale, 1977). The state provides the framework of law which enables the BBC and IBA to broadcast at all, and it provides journalists with more news material than any other single source. At the same time, modern governments depend on television for opportunities to disseminate their arguments and policies. Maintaining this delicate balance, by formal and informal means, is a continuous process, which periodically erupts into open conflict.

The government defends itself against the press through a combination of secrecy, management of news, and censorship. The secrecy of the British state, epitomised in the Official Secrets Act, is notorious. Section 2 of the 1911 Act says, essentially, that any information obtained as a result of employment by the Crown or the government is secret unless it has been declared not to be. News management is conducted mainly through ministerial press officers, who hold regular press conferences and briefings. These occasions are managed by government to ensure that the best possible version of events is put forward, and are essential sources of information.

Full-blown censorship means that an agency of the state has power to vet every item of news before publication, and to ban it at that point. Material can also be censored after publication, by seizing it and punishing those responsible. The threat of subsequent prosecution can be as effective as prior censorship, especially when, as in Britain, the law is vague as to what would or would not be prosecuted. Prior censorship is rare in Britain in peacetime, though it occurred during the Falklands conflict, but something very like it occurred when police seized materials relating to a proposed TV series about the security services. Less formally, governments have been known to approach both BBC and IBA with a 'request' not to broadcast material, as in the *Real Lives* affair.

The best-known of the semi-formal systems of control are 'D' ('Defence') notices, which are sent by ministers to editors, requesting them not to publish material that would not be 'in the national interest'. The system is rarely used and has no legal backing, but it generally works, partly because journalists recognise that there are legitimate reasons for it, and partly because of the sanctions that can be brought against journalists who ignore a notice – that government sources will not co-operate with them in the future. 'D' notices amount to voluntary censorship.

It is in the system of informal constraints that the interdependence of state and media becomes apparent. Ministers need journalists, as we have seen, but they also know the power of the media to destroy a political career, or even a government. Journalists need the co-operation of ministers if they are to keep the public informed about government, but know that those they may wish to criticise are their most important source of information.

Most of the 'insider' information that journalists really value comes from two main sources, 'leaks' and 'the lobby'. Political leaks are not accidental. They are controlled releases of information through which members of the government ensure that information reaches the public via the media, but is not attributed to a particular source.

The lobby is more routinised. It is a group of political correspondents who have the right to stand in the lobby of the House of Commons, button-holing MPs, especially backbenchers, and obtaining their views, usually attributable. They are an elite, who receive copies of official publications before they are publicly available, sometimes even before MPs get them.

They have an office in the Palace of Westminister and are invited to attend briefings held by ministerial staff, especially those of the prime minister, as well as weekly meetings with the leader of the house and with the leader of the opposition.

Membership of the lobby confers privileged access to sources in Westminister and Downing Street, so members are most unlikely to risk their position by broadcasting material which they know will result in the loss of that position.

Though the Northern Ireland conflict has for the last 20 years been one of the most tightly controlled areas of news reporting, there is still very little formal censorship, in the sense of directives or bans by government, which is why this ban has received so much attention. But there hardly needs to be censorship, for both government and media know the informal rules and the system is self-regulating. 'There is no need to police a mass medium that is itself so well-regulated that it never steps out of line. The arsenal of powers that the state is able to deploy against the media is for the most part kept in reserve . . . a deterrent to deviance and a spur to self-control' (Barrat, 1986).

4 NOVEMBER 1988

Discussion Topic

In what circumstances can censorship be justified?

FURTHER READING

Barrat, D. (1986) *Media Sociology* (Tavistock).

Munro, C. (1979) *Television Censorship and the Law* (Saxon House).

Whale, J. (1977) *The Politics of the Media* (Fontana).

28
Figuring out the NHS

Understanding Health Spending

The condition of the National Health Service has long been a favourite target for critics of the government, whoever is in power. Allegations of neglect and underfunding, or of wastage and extravagance, always supported by impressive-looking figures, have been countered with the support of other equally impressive statistics.

So it was predictable that the Chancellor's announcement in November 1988 that an additional £2bn is to be spent on the NHS over the next year would be welcomed by Tory back benchers and belittled by the opposition. On the government's figures, NHS spending in England will total nearly £20bn in 1989/90, a real increase of 4.5 per cent on the previous year, and a near fourfold increase since 1975. But there are still long waiting-lists and shortages of staff and equipment. How can this be?

Arguments about the quality of the NHS which are based simply on the amount of money being spent on it make for easy political exchanges, but are of little value in making a proper assessment of the situation. This requires us to distinguish between the amount of money being spent, the amount of activity going on, and the benefits resulting therefrom. Increasing the amount of money being spent on such items as staff, equipment, drugs etc. does not automatically mean that the service being provided is any better. This has to be measured separately, in terms of things like how many people pass through the system in a year, and how many treatments are given.

But even this does not provide a measure of the real test of a health care delivery system: whether the health of individuals or of the community is better than it was before. This outcome is notoriously difficult to measure, but must be the critical test of the system, particularly since it was the explicit goal when the NHS was first set up. The National Health Service Act, passed in 1946 and implemented in 1948, stated that its aim was to 'secure improvement in the physical and mental health of the people and the prevention, diagnosis and treatment of illness'. The intention was to make good health care available to the whole population without any financial barriers.

With the wisdom of hindsight, it is easy to fault the founders of the NHS. They anticipated that, as the health of the nation improved, so the demand for health services would decrease. It is now clear that this simple demand/supply model is inadequate, and that the NHS cannot be considered in isolation from its wider social context. Butler and Vaile (1984) identify five dimensions of this wider context: the demographic, the epidemiological, the cultural, the economic, and the political.

Economic factors affect both supply and demand. The general state of the national economy is related in all countries to how much is spent on health care, and also affects the cost of staff, drugs, equipment, and treatments. Since the price of medical services tends to rise faster than prices generally, partly because of rising labour costs and partly because of the development of new but increasingly expensive treatments, there is an endless demand for more cash simply to maintain the supply of services. There are also links between sickness rates and economic conditions. Unemployment, for example, damages your health.

The political context is mainly a supply factor, and has again been of central importance in recent years, with the government favouring what Trowler (1984) calls the 'Market Liberal' view of how health care should be provided, and the opposition favouring a 'Social Democratic' model. The latter stresses that government has a moral duty to make provision for health and welfare, while the Market Liberal approach argues that market forces should regulate the provision of these services, as in the introduction of higher charges for dental and optician services. Most health care should, they argue, be provided via the private not the public sector.

The other three factors all tend to increase demand for health care. In the 1950s and 1960s, the main demographic feature was the rise in the birth-rate, with consequent extra spending on ante-natal, natal and post-natal care. As the birth-rate fell from its peak in the 1960s, this area of expenditure decreased relative to the rest, only to be replaced by ever-increasing expenditure on the elderly, as their numbers have grown.

Epidemiological changes refer to changes in the extent and patterns of distribution of disease. For example, though the infectious diseases of childhood have been largely brought under control, mainly through relatively inexpensive immunisation programmes, cancer and heart disease are more common, and are expensive to treat. The most recent 'new' disease is Aids, which has attracted considerable funding, which will therefore be unavailable for other areas.

Relevant cultural changes include those concerned with people's attitudes and lifestyles, which are also related to economic factors. Improved housing and nutrition have led to better health, and the decrease in smoking will certainly save the NHS money in the long run, as will healthier eating. At the same time, the increase in car ownership and traffic accidents results in rising costs, as does the increase in diseases related to atmospheric pollution. Stress, at home or at work, damages people's physical as well as their mental health.

Another cultural change is people's greater expectations of what medicine can do. Today, people expect treatment for conditions that their grandparents would have had to tolerate as part of the human condition. This is partly the result of real advances made in medical treatments but is also a result of the medical profession's own ideology. The image of doctors as all-powerful and all-knowing has led to people coming to believe that this is true and to demand cures for more ills than medicine can in fact cope with.

Two billion pounds is a lot of money, but how far it will help to 'secure improvement in the physical and mental health of the people' is not just a matter of calculating percentages.

18 NOVEMBER 1988

Discussion Topic

How far do the five factors identified apply also to the provision of education, or housing?

FURTHER READING

Butler, J. and Vaile, M. (1984) *Health and Health Services* (RKP).
Trowler, P. (1984) *Topics in Sociology* (UTP).

29

Sacred Cows

Can Morality be Absolute?

'My list of rights and wrongs are not just middle-class values – they are classless values . . . . They are not just Conservative values – they are universal values . . . . They are not just traditional values – they are essential values for any civilised society'. In these terms, in a speech on 8 November 1988, Education Secretary Kenneth Baker made his case for claiming that there are moral principles and values that are right for all places, all people and all societies at all times.

He specified eight such values, four 'wrongs' and four 'rights'. The 'wrongs' were: 'It is wrong to lie; it is wrong to steal; it is wrong to cheat; it is wrong to bully'. The 'rights' included: 'It is right to respect your elders' and 'It is right to help those less fortunate and those weaker than ourselves'. Baker argued that these universal values have been undermined since the 1960s, and that 'the handmaidens of this revolution were those social scientists and the counter-culture prophets who so eagerly propagated excuses for the inexcusable. Concepts of right and wrong became blurred . . .'

One issue over which we could engage with Baker is that he confuses the explaining of actions with the condoning of them. It is perfectly possible to understand actions while condemning them on moral grounds (see Article 36). For the moment, we will concern ourselves with the issue of moral relativism, that is, with the question of whether morals and values can be absolute, or whether they are valid only for the age in which they are held, or for the people by whom they are held.

First, Baker's comments can be questioned on historical grounds. He suggests that 'values became relative' in the 1960s, and that this was the result of certain kinds of social science. In fact, the philosophical debate about moral relativism dates back at least to the ancient Greeks, can be found in the 16th and 17th centuries (Montaigne, Locke), and was revived in the 19th century in the light of early anthropological work.

Next, such empirical research has shown many times that actions which are regarded as right in one society are considered wrong in another. An unusual example, recorded by both Chagnon and Shapiro, is how the male Yanomamo Indians of Brazil all physically abuse their wives. Kind husbands merely bruise and mutilate; fierce ones wound and kill. Chagnon states that Yanomamo women measure their status as wives by the frequency of their beatings.

Similarly, the same action may be regarded as right by one social group and wrong by others in the same society. The defence of territory, or of 'ends' at football grounds, by the use of violence, provides an example in our society. This is not just a case of one group being more tolerant of wrong-doing than another, but of a real difference of opinion about when the use of violence is justified.

What is morally acceptable in a society also varies over time. The degree of physical violence that can be acceptably used to discipline children has changed drastically in our society in recent years. The principle of 'Spare the rod and spoil the child' has been replaced by new definitions of what constitutes assault on the person. Such variations prompt the question 'on what grounds can it be argued that one set of moral values is better than another?'. Baker claims that his set of values is universal and essential, and so superior, but his list poses major philosophical problems.

The claim that the value 'It is wrong to steal' is universal has the key weakness that such statements are true by definition. The words 'steal', 'lie', 'cheat' and 'bully' all imply moral wrong. To say 'It is wrong to steal' is simply to say 'It is morally wrong to take something in a morally wrong way', and so is correct but tautological (saying the same thing twice but in different words). It does not help in identifying whether any particular act is theft.

Similarly, all members of all societies would agree that 'It is wrong to commit murder', because 'murder' means 'morally wrong killing'. The moral disagreement and variation arises over what actions should be classified as 'murder'. The person who kills for revenge in a Sicilian vendetta will regard the act as not only morally right but morally required. He will agree that murder is wrong, but will not include revenge killing in that category. From Baker's list, all the four 'wrongs' are the same sort of self-evident truths. There is still the problem of how to decide which actions count as lying, stealing, cheating and bullying.

Baker's four 'rights' are, in contrast, not tautological. 'It is right to respect your elders' is a moral statement which has to be argued for, because it is not true by definition but brings together two concepts, 'elderly' and 'respect' which have no necessary logical connection. Even if the case is successfully made, it is not clear what form respecting should take. Is it a sign of respect to do as the nomadic Eskimo used to do, and leave their elderly to die in the cold, after due ceremonies of farewell, or is it a mark of respect to do as we do, and keep some of our elderly alive to a stage where they lose dignity?

Similarly, 'It is right to help those less fortunate and those weaker than ourselves' is in accord with Christian, Islamic and other religious teachings, but it still has to be argued for, as it is not self-evidently true. I might agree with it; you might agree with it; Baker obviously does agree with it, at least in theory, but this unanimity does not make it a universal value, just a widely accepted one. And this leaves open the question of who is 'less fortunate' and who is to blame for their situation, who is 'weaker', and what constitutes 'help'. The same problems apply to 'It is right to know that you can't have everything you want instantly' and 'It is right to take personal responsibility for your actions'.

In showing that moral values vary from one social context to another, social scientists have not undermined morality, but have invigorated the philosophical debate about whether absolute morals are logically possible. Over centuries, philosophers have suggested various grounds on which absolute moral correctness might be claimed. Simple assertion is not one of them.

16 DECEMBER 1988

Discussion Topic

When are we justified in imposing our values on others?

FURTHER READING

Harris, M. (1977) *Cows, Pigs, Wars and Witches* (Fontana).

30

Spend, Spend, Spend . . .

Poverty in Britain Today

Christmas, in the UK at least, is a time for conspicuous consumption. Huge amounts are spent on frivolous goods, as well as on food and drink. But not everybody participates in this orgy of spending.

Two stories, printed beside each other in our local free newspaper, make the point neatly. The first, illustrated with a photograph, tells the reader that a local shop has for sale a seven-foot-high toy polar bear, which is priced at £2200 by the shopowner, who also has two full-size toy sheep-dogs permanently in the back of his Range Rover. The story next to it concerns three Bangladeshi families who are threatened with eviction from their bed and breakfast accommodation because the local authority has decided that they have made themselves homeless intentionally.

Such a contrast starkly illustrates the nature of inequality and poverty in Britain today. As explained in an earlier article (No. 13) poverty in the UK is best understood as a matter of relative deprivation rather than of absolute poverty, as that is experienced in parts of the Third World. To be poor in Britain is to have resources of income and wealth so far below the norm that you are unable fully to participate in social, economic and political life. Such relative poverty is the more keenly felt at times when the majority are spending freely. The more unequal the distribution of income and wealth; the greater such contrasts become.

Valid and reliable statistics about economic inequality are difficult to produce, but *Social Trends* is a widely-accepted source. The 1987 edition shows that inequalities of income have widened in the 1980s, to the point where, in 1984, the bottom fifth of the population received 6.7 per cent of income after taxes, while the top fifth received 39.7 per cent. The distribution of personal wealth is even more unequal: the top 1 per cent of the population owned over one fifth of the total marketable wealth, while the bottom 50 per cent shared among themselves only 7 per cent of the total.

It is undeniable that overall standards of living in the UK are rising, but they are rising faster for the better-off than for the poor, so the gap is widening. Taking the poverty line to be supplementary benefit rates (income support from 1988), the Child Poverty Action Group calculated that, in 1985, 29 per cent of the population of Great Britain, or about 15.5 million people, were living at 140 per cent of supplementary benefit level or below. In 1988 income support terms, that means an income, after housing costs are met, of less than £36.47 per week for a single person under 25, or £110.74 for a two-parent family with two children under 11.

So who are the people most likely to be in poverty in Britain today? When Peter Townsend and Brian Abel-Smith published *The Poor and the Poorest* in 1965, reopening the poverty debate after a long period of public complacency, they identified the five main groups in poverty as being fatherless families, the unemployed, the low-paid, sick and disabled people and pensioners. In 1989, the same five groups are at risk, the difference being that all these groups are now larger, and that the proportions of each within the whole have changed.

Of the total poor today, just over a third are pensioners, about a quarter are unemployed, about one in five are low-paid people in full-time work, about 4 per cent are sick or disabled, and the rest are single parents, students, people temporarily off work, and people caring for dependent relatives.

Despite this amount of detail, the statistics still fail to give us a full picture of the real victims of poverty. Research has tended to measure poverty in terms of families and households, which conceals how the effects of poverty fall unequally within these social units.

Women, for instance, suffer from poverty more than men, since they outnumber men in nearly all the five groups listed above. Given their greater life-expectancy, women make up the majority of pensioners. The number of one-parent families has increased from 8 per cent of all families with dependent children in 1971 to 14 per cent in 1987, and nine out of ten of these families are headed by women. Similarly, most of those who care for dependent relatives are women. While the majority of the registered unemployed are men, the types of unemployment which are not fully recognised in the official statistics fall disproportionately on women. Low-paid work is substantially done by women, whose average wage remains remorselessly at about two-thirds of the average for men.

An even more hidden aspect of women's poverty is that, in households with children where the gross family income is low, it is usually the mother who will 'go without'.

Ethnic minorities, too, may suffer disproportionately from poverty. While it is true that there are still relatively few people of pensionable age among the ethnic minorities, they certainly suffer more from unemployment and low pay. The consequences of poverty, such as poor housing, higher rates of illness and a lower life expectancy are all part of the experience of members of the ethnic minorities.

And what is the cause of poverty in the five groups? Do they have anything in common? The important point to recognise is that it is not being old or sick or not in employment that causes poverty. If it were, the Queen Mother, for example, would be poor. The cause of poverty in the elderly is having had a job without an occupational pension and with a wage that precluded substantial saving, or never having had stable employment at all. If being a single parent or being disabled were causes of poverty in a straightforward sense, then all single parents and all disabled people would be poor, and they are not.

The Child Poverty Action Group summarises the situation thus: 'People become poor in this country because either they work for a poverty wage or, unable to work and lacking capital assets to produce an unearned income, they become dependent on inadequate state benefits'.

6 JANUARY 1989

Discussion Topic

How were the material benefits of Christmas distributed in your household?

FURTHER READING

Child Poverty Action Group (1988) *Poverty; the Facts* (CPAG).

31

Whose Time is it Anyway?

The Concept of Time

'I had a really good Christmas holiday. I completely lost track of time. It's hard to get back to the old routine'. Remarks like this reveal something of how we think about time, and how closely our concept of it is related to work. We feel that a holiday is not really a holiday if we keep having to think about what day of the week it is, and that work is not really work unless it is governed by the clock. Like all complex industrial societies, ours is one where time, as measured and recorded by the clock, the diary and the wall calendar, is a key governing principle of our lives.

Both anthropology and history illustrate that it was not always so. In his celebrated study of the Nuer, Evans-Pritchard states that they 'have no expression equivalent to "time" in our language, and they cannot therefore, as we can, speak of time as though it were something actual, which passes, can be wasted, can be saved, and so forth'.

He describes how the Nuer daily round is organised not in terms of an abstract notion of what time it is, but in terms of the regular tasks, 'generally of a leisurely nature, that are performed in caring for the cattle'. Daily activities such as milking, driving cattle to pasture, cleaning the byre and so on, all take place in the same order each day, and the Nuer do not 'experience the same feeling of fighting against time or of having to coordinate activities with an abstract passage of time'. Evans-Pritchard comments, rather wistfully, that 'the Nuer are fortunate'.

Evans-Pritchard in 1940 was describing what has since come to be called 'cyclical time', which is contrasted with 'linear time'. Cyclical time, which Young (1988) also calls 'natural time', is marked by the seasons of the year, by the sun rising, passing across the sky and setting, by the phases of the moon, by the body's daily rhythms, and by any event which recurs regularly and recognisably. It emphasises continuity and hence reassurance. Linear time, or 'bureaucratic time', involves a notion of time passing in a continuous flow and at a constant speed, with no one moment ever being repeated. It implies progress, change and development. But it also creates the familiar sense of being under pressure of time, of being rushed, and of having too much to do in the time available.

All cultures, of course, have some notion of daily, lunar and annual cycles, but many make no abstract linear sub-divisions of time into weeks, hours or minutes of fixed length. Instead, periods of time are specified in terms of how long it takes to complete an activity, for example 'a rice-cooking' in Madagascar, or a cigarette-smoking in wartime Crete.

Young (1988) and Thompson (1967) argue, from different perspectives, that our society places too much emphasis on abstract linear time and has lost sight of the continuing importance of cyclical time. Thompson shows how pre-industrial society, whose economic activities are largely dependent on natural cycles, tends to conceive of time in terms of 'task-orientation'.

Even in our society today a fishing community will have its life governed by the times of the tides, rather than by clock-time. Similarly, working from dawn to dusk is appropriate in farming communities at harvest-time, or at lambing. No one in such a community will say 'It's five o'clock. I'm knocking off for the day'. Thompson describes how the clock came to play a central role in the social and economic life of Western Europe from the 17th century onwards (though the sundial remained in use into the 19th century), and how the restructuring of working habits that accompanied the industrial revolution influenced the way in which working people came to conceive of time.

He argues that 'as soon as actual hands are employed, the shift from task-orientation to timed labour is marked', for employment introduces a division in the minds of employees between their employer's time and their 'own' time. Time becomes a currency to be spent.

Through the 18th and 19th centuries, pocket-watches became not only useful, but also conferred prestige upon the owner. Even today a long-serving employee may be given, upon retirement, an engraved gold watch or a mantel clock. The more that work becomes specialised and sub-divided between different workers and work-places, the more co-ordination is required. Clock-time becomes an essential part of the production and distribution processes.

Industrial societies, then, whose economic activities are relatively independent of natural cycles, operate with a linear concept of time. Where electricity is universally available, work and leisure schedules can ignore the rising and the setting of the sun. In such societies, time is measured very precisely, in abstract terms, and by the clock.

Young (1988) also argues that we attach too much importance to linear time. We tend to belittle the cyclical as being acceptable to ancient societies and superstitions but not to scientific future-oriented societies like ours. He maintains, though, that cyclical time is still very important, and that the two co-exist and are interdependent. He identifies a conflict between natural rhythms and the rhythms of industrial society, but believes that this conflict can be reduced or removed. 'Machine-like cycles in a metronomic society do not have to be the lot of human beings forever'.

He describes the daily, lunar and annual cycles, both physical and social, of mankind and of other organisms and natural processes. He looks for a sociological clock to parallel our biological clock, and finds it in the force of habit and custom, and the tendency to do again what we have done before. In this way continuity and hence social structure is maintained, while continually changing.

'Most people', Young says, 'relish the recurring festivals of the year'. The Christmas holiday derives much of its attraction from its reassuringly cyclical nature, and from the way in which linear time is temporarily suspended, returning us, however briefly, to a world where we control time rather than it controlling us.

13 JANUARY 1989

Discussion Topic

Distinguish between the cyclical aspects and the linear aspects of your educational career.

FURTHER READING

Thompson, E.P. (1967) 'Time, Work-Discipline and Industrial Capitalism', *Past and Present 38.*

Young, M. (1988) *The Metronomic Society* (Thames & Hudson).

32

A Good Judge?

The Social Background of the Judiciary

It sometimes seems that there is an endless supply of judges willing and able to create a furore about their comments in court and the sentences they hand down to convicted criminals. In the case of Judge Harold Cassel, the controversy at the end of November 1988 centred on the leniency of the sentence (two years' probation) he imposed on a man who had sexually assaulted his 12-year-old step-daughter, and on the comments the judge made at the time, which suggested that the man had been to some extent driven to the act because of his pregnant wife's 'lack of sexual appetite'. Judge Cassel resigned shortly afterwards.

On other occasions, it has been the severity of a sentence that has attracted criticism, and it is worth noting that Judge Cassel's sentence was handed out at a time when judges have in general been imposing longer prison sentences than they did a few years ago. But the central issues underlying controversies about the severity or leniency of sentences are the same: the power, discretion and possible bias of the judiciary. Research has shown repeatedly that there are considerable variations in the sentencing policies of different courts, including magistrates' courts. One study quoted in Hall (1987) showed that, in 12 different courts, the use of the prison sentence for comparable property offences ranged from 15 to 50 per cent.

In the case involving Judge Cassel, critics argued that his leniency reflected a form of male bias. Judge Cassel was not only male but also conformed to the stereotype of judges in other ways: old (72), white, and with a public school, Oxbridge and army background. Data from Labour Research in January 1987 shows that, of 465 judges, 464 were white, 448 were male, 166 were over 65, and the great majority had very privileged backgrounds. According to *New Society* in May 1970, 81 per cent of judges had been to public schools and 76 per cent to Oxbridge.

Clearly this social background cannot automatically be linked to any particular political view or bias, any more than coming from a lower socio-economic background necessarily means that someone will be anti-establishment. In either case, we need to be aware of the importance of occupational socialisation in the formation and reinforcement of attitudes. Writing of the 30 or so most powerful policy-making judges, Griffith (1985) argues that they have 'by their education and training and the pursuit of their profession as barristers, acquired a strikingly homogeneous collection of attitudes, beliefs and principles, which to them represents the public interest'.

As an example, Griffith claims that judges are more enthusiastic in defending property rights than wider human rights or personal liberties. Thus, in cases involving squatters in empty properties, the squatters – typically young and poor, and facing a serious housing shortage – were usually given short shrift. Griffith also argues that judges have tended to look less favourably on claims to social rights, such as when interpreting anti-discrimination legislation, or collective rights, as in trade unionism, than they have on rights claimed by individuals.

The phrase 'the public interest' is important because it reminds us that judges not only sentence criminals but are involved in legal judgments about industrial relations, political protest, race relations, government secrecy, police powers and sexual behaviour. They do not simply administer the law in a passive way. There is much potential for judges to make law when interpreting it.

In addition to this, there is the common law, which is based on decisions by courts over the centuries that have become precedents. These are binding on subsequent judgments, though there is no parliamentary statute. On every occasion where such issues have come before the courts in the last 30 years, says Griffith, 'the judges have supported the conventional, established, settled interests'.

As a conflict theorist, Griffith rejects the idea that there is a single public interest, maintaining instead that different social classes and groups have different interests. The judiciary, he says, uphold dominant interests but, by doing this in the name of impartiality and the rule of law, they give legitimacy to the established system of power.

Griffith is not arguing that it is simply or primarily the background of judges or their personal qualities that leads to this situation. Instead, he favours a structuralist approach that sees judicial bias as stemming from the very nature and role of the judiciary as part of the machinery of authority and government. A more pluralist view regards judicial policy as being more diverse and less predictable. Griffith's critics argue that he exaggerates the extent of judicial consistency in the areas he studies, such as industrial relations. There is evidence of disagreement between judges, as in cases of split decisions, or of decisions being reversed on appeal to a higher court.

Stuart Hall believes that the evidence on judicial consistency supports Griffith's argument. From a Marxist standpoint, however, he emphasises the role of the judiciary in capitalist societies, and rejects Griffith's argument that this role will be more or less the same in all types of society. He is particularly interested in the way that judicial policy may be influenced by prevailing ideologies. This version of Marxism draws on Gramsci's theory of hegemony (see Article 25) and is concerned with the way that legal judgments can reinforce certain ideas about how society should be organised.

Looking again at the case which involved Judge Cassel, we can see how such judgments, if left unchallenged, reinforce certain ideas about the family, sexuality, masculinity, and the role of women in marriage. For example, it sets boundaries for fathers' rights over their daughters, and perhaps for both parents over all their children, in a way which seems to accept some degree of exploitation. It appears to give priority to male sexual rights over those of others. Would the sentence have been the same if the victim had been unrelated to the assailant?

20 JANUARY 1989

Discussion Topic

What factors do you think should influence judges in sentencing offenders in cases such as this?

FURTHER READING

Griffith, J. (1985) *The Politics of the Judiciary*, 3rd ed.

Hall, S. (1987) *Delivering Justice*, parts 2a and 2b (Open University Press).

33

Latest Trends

The Registrar-General's Scale of Social Class

January is a good month for anyone interested in the state of the nation, at least in a sociological sense, for it sees the annual publication of *Britain: an Official Handbook* and *Social Trends*, both from HMSO. These two include essential data for social scientists, but *Social Trends* in particular is not only a resource, it also provides plenty of good topics for sociological analysis.

One of these is classification. Many of the tables are presented in categories such as age and gender, and many, especially those derived from the General Household Survey, are classified according to a scale of social class. There are several such scales but the oldest, whose basic pattern is followed by all the others, is the Registrar-General's (RG), first used in the 1911 census.

During the second half of the 19th century, analysis of census returns and of the figures for births and deaths had revealed substantial differences in the mortality rates, especially those for infant mortality, of workers in different occupations. It had also been shown that the upper classes enjoyed greater life expectancy than the general population, and that the greatest gap occurred in infancy and childhood. The improvement in adult mortality from the 1840s was not reflected in infant mortality.

The 1911 scale was devised primarily as an instrument to help in the analysis of infant mortality. The population was divided into eight groups of which only the first five were ranked in descending order. Social Class 1 was 'the upper and middle classes', III was 'skilled occupations', II was 'intermediate' between I and III, V was 'unskilled occupations' and IV was 'intermediate' between III and V. The other three groups – textile workers, miners, and agricultural workers – were analysed separately. Occupations were placed in each category, not on the basis of their infant mortality rates, but according to their degree of skill and their standing. However, subsequent analysis of the census and of registration statistics for each class revealed marked gradients in both mortality and fertility.

Though the 1911 scale has been amended and refined, its basic structure has been retained ever since. In 1970, for example, Class III was divided into two (III non-manual and III manual), making it possible to combine the resulting six classes into non-manual and manual workers. The scale is now:

I.   Professional (e.g. doctors, solicitors, architects).
II.   Managerial and lower professional (e.g. sales managers, school-teachers, MPs, nurses).
III(N).   Non-manual skilled (e.g. clerks, shop assistants).
III(M).   Skilled manual (e.g. bricklayers, hairdressers, butchers).
IV.   Partly skilled (e.g. bus conductors, postal workers, packers).
V.   Unskilled occupations (e.g. porters, labourers).

Full-time students and people whose occupation is 'inadequately described' plus, since 1961, members of the armed forces are excluded from the classification.

The RG's scale was originally based on the subjective judgment of the RG, or rather of a certain Dr Stevenson. Other widely used scales, such as that devised by Hall and Jones in the late 1940s or by Hope and Goldthorpe for the Oxford Mobility Study in the 1970s, are the results of sample surveys asking people how they rank occupation in order of status. But all three scales reflect similar values, such as that non-manual work is superior to manual work. Marxists would reject this view and argue that any such scale ignores the tensions and conflict between those at the top and those at the bottom of the class structure.

Besides these important theoretical issues, there are problems with the RG's scale in its own terms. For instance, changes in the training needs and the social standing of some occupations has resulted in their class being changed, with a loss of comparability of the statistics over the years. The half-million male clerks in RGI in 1911 were in RGIII by 1931. Airline pilots and actors rose from RGIII to RGII in 1960, and university teachers were promoted from RGII to RGI. The scale takes no account of income, earned or unearned, which means that some people in RGII for example, such as nurses, have lower incomes than some of the skilled manual workers of RGIII(M). The wealthy minority, whose income is derived from substantial ownership of capital, do not feature in the scale at all.

In addition, there are problems with the reliability of the raw data. While data collected from the census is more reliable than that collected through registration of births and deaths, there is still a tendency to upgrade occupations or to describe them too briefly. 'Company director' can mean many things.

There is a big problem with the ranking of married women, who are assumed to be in the same social class as their husband. While this assumption was not too misleading in 1911, it is thoroughly question-able in the 1980s. A particular discrepancy is that married women classified by their own occupation are concentrated in RGIII(N), whereas, when they are classified with their husbands, they are concentrated in RGIII(M). A number of studies in recent years have produced separate figures for women, and there is a strong case for making this the norm.

The size of the classes varies also from one age group to another, as employment patterns change. It is important, when looking at these tables, to check which age groups are included (especially children and retired people), whether the unemployed (allocated to their last job) have been included, and how women have been classified.

Whatever its shortcomings, though, the RG's scale reveals the per-sistence of correlations between occupation and inequalities of health, life expectancy, housing conditions, disposable income, hours of work, length and standard of education, age at marriage, size of family, church attendance, leisure interests, newspaper readership and TV watching, political involvement and a dozen other characteristics. Occupation is not the same thing as class, but it remains an excellent predictor of life-chances.

27 JANUARY 1989

Discussion Topic

'If people stopped going on about it, class would wither away'. Do you agree?

FURTHER READING

Reid, I. (1981) *Social Class Differences in Britain* (Grant McIntyre).

34

To Honour and Obey?

Power and Authority

George Bush is one of the most powerful men in the world. But what is the origin of his power, what are its limits, and how does it differ from other kinds of power?

Power is involved in virtually every social relationship, whether between two individuals or nation-states. Disagreements and clashes of interest arise in every relationship and have to be resolved if the relationship is to continue. Sometimes this is achieved through negotiation between two parties of equal standing but, more usually, one party is in a stronger position to get its way.

Max Weber defined power as 'the probability that one actor in a social relationship will be able to carry out his will in the pursuit of goals of action, despite resistance'. In its most basic form, the exercise of power depends on being able to use force. Thus the power of the playground bully has a similar basis to that of the nation-state with superior armed forces. Often the threat rather than the actual use of force is enough.

In most situations, however, whether at work or at leisure, one person obeys another not because they are frightened, but because they accept the right of that person to give instructions. For Weber, this is the difference between power and authority: authority is legitimate or morally justifiable power, power that one person acknowledges another's right to exercise. In the context of the authority of the state, Weber identified three kinds of legitimate authority: traditional, rational-legal, and charismatic, which he described in ideal-type terms.

Traditional authority is based on 'an established belief in the sanctity of immemorial traditions and the legitimacy of those exercising authority under them'. People obey rules and those who enforce the rules because 'it's always been done like that'. In political terms, this kind of authority is sometimes associated with a gerontocracy, i.e. rule by old people, whose authority is based on the belief that their age gives them wisdom. Or it may be the basis of the authority of someone who has inherited the position of head of state, such as the absolute monarch in a feudal system. Similarly, regarding the father as head of the family is based on traditional patriarchal values.

Rational-legal authority involves 'a belief in the legality of enacted rules and the right of those elevated to authority under such rules to issue commands'. Rules are obeyed because they are seen as having been created legally, such as through parliamentary process, and people are obeyed because of the position they occupy in a properly-established hierarchy. It is the position that is obeyed rather than the person occupying it. Rules are impersonal and apply universally to everybody. Weber argued that modern societies have discarded traditional patterns of authority and developed rational-legal institutions.

The most developed example of rational action and organisation is found in bureaucracies, about which Weber wrote extensively. In his ideal-type of bureaucracy, instructions are legitimate when they are given by the correct official according to the correct procedures. If an instruction is given through a wrong procedure, or by the wrong official, then it has no legitimacy and will not, in the ideal type, be obeyed. The smooth running of a bureaucracy depends on agreement that its rules of procedure are rational and fair.

Charismatic authority is based on 'a certain quality of an individual personality by virtue of which he is considered extraordinary and treated as endowed with supernatural, super-human, or at least specifically exceptional powers or qualities'. Many religious sects have been based on the charismatic authority of an individual leader, of whom Jesus Christ is an obvious example, though charisma is not only possessed by good people. Adolf Hitler and Charles Manson share this quality with Mother Theresa and the prophet Muhammad.

Typically, a charismatic leader will attract a band of disciples who enjoy some reflected authority. When the leader dies, these disciples may disband, or they may convert the basis of the authority into traditional (e.g. the leader's son succeeds) or legal arrangements (e.g. an administrative apparatus is set up).

Charismatic authority is temporary and unstable and must be routinised if it is to survive the death of the figurehead. Fidel Castro, for example, though his initial authority rested at least in part on his charisma when leading the Cuban revolution, now increasingly relies on rational-legal authority. Weber maintained that charisma is a creative force in history, and may emerge as a reaction against bureaucracies which have become too rigid.

Weber's categories of legitimate authority are ideal types. That is to say, they are neither descriptions of a perfect situation nor of an actual reality. They are ideal in the sense of being theoretical, and should be used as fixed standards or guides with which to compare real situations. Thus George Bush's authority, at least on the domestic front, rests on a blend of all three types. It is predominantly rational-legal, in that he has been elected publicly according to a set of rules which has been demonstrably observed. President Nixon, in contrast, was forced to resign when the Watergate affair revealed that he had broken the rules.

Mr Bush's legitimacy among urban black Americans is more in doubt, as there is evidence of widespread rejection of the political system itself. His authority also has traditional elements, much being made of the fact that he is the 41st president in a line that is continuous from George Washington. No one could pretend that Mr Bush has much personal charisma, but he will benefit from the charisma of the office. The media will go on playing a key role in creating his image.

In matters of foreign policy his legitimacy is more questionable, as America's enemies, and many of her allies, deny his claim to the right to intervene in their affairs. On the world stage, Mr Bush's ability to get his own way will depend more on power than on authority.

3 FEBRUARY 1989

Discussion Topic

Take three examples of people in authority over you, and discuss the basis of that authority.

FURTHER READING

Lukes, S. (1979) 'Power and Authority', in T. Bottomore and Nisbet, R. *A History of Sociological Analysis* (H.E.B.).

35

Halcyon Days

The Sociology of Communes

As many students know, sixties nostalgia flourishes among middle-aged sociologists. Before you know it, the standard lesson on the sociology of youth culture becomes a session of reminiscence of happy days of student protest, of hippies and flower-power.

From time to time, echoes of those supposedly halcyon days are heard, as in the High Court hearing in 1989 when the Rainbow Tribe of Dyfed lost their appeal against the Secretary of State's order to dismantle the tepees in which they live, on the grounds that they are in breach of planning regulations. The Rainbow Tribe have occupied their 70-acre site since 1976, trying to recreate the life-style of the North American Indians, but their roots lie in the counter-culture of the 1960s.

Communalism was not an invention of the sixties. An example of an early commune was that of the Diggers, a group of about 20 poor people who argued that the English Civil War had been fought against king and landowners and that, now that the war was won, land should be made available to the poor. They assembled at St George's Hill in Surrey in March 1649 and began to cultivate the common land. This aroused the hostility of the Commonwealth government and of local landowners, and within a year the Diggers had been dispersed. The Paris Commune of 1871 provides another example, as do religious groups like Oneida and the Amish in the US, and the kibbutzim of Israel.

The surge of interest in the 1960s reflected several of the strands of thinking that made up the 'counter-culture'. These included a view of the family as a repressive institution that damaged personal growth; the questioning of traditional attitudes towards marriage and sexuality; the reinvigoration of feminist thinking; a rejection of technology, urbanism and industrialism, combined with a strong attraction to the land; a search for a more authentic self and for deeper human relationships; a growing interest in astrological and New Age ideas; and a desire for greater egalitarianism. The commune, especially the self-sufficient rural commune, seemed to offer a way of life able to respond to all these.

Findhorn, probably still the largest British commune, was founded in Morayshire in 1962 with a strong spiritual orientation. In 1967 Sid Rawle, now associated with the Peace Convoy, founded the British Diggers, who later moved to an island off the west coast of Ireland given to them by John Lennon. The London Street Commune concentrated on squatting in central London. The number of communes seems to have fluctuated between 40 and 100 during this period, but with a rapid turnover.

Abrams and McCulloch (1976) is a study of communes using a combination of a questionnaire-based survey, accounts provided by members of communes, and ethnographic studies of 67 communes. McCulloch later wrote that:

'These new forms of households are all decidedly middle-class in orientation and social composition . . . [they] . . . take many forms but the ideological hallmark of their collective project is the attempt to create a form of intimate existence characterised by openness and non-exclusive attachments.'

They were, however, very unstable. Of the 67 studied over four years, only six survived that period.

While stressing the dangers, even the impossibility, of making valid generalisations about communes, Abrams and McCulloch identified two models. 'Communal households' involved each individual sharing their lives with all other members of the household. In 'collective households', by contrast, the basic unit remained the nuclear family, with each family sharing resources such as a house and land but retaining its own identity. 'Friendship is communal but intimacy is private'. In practice, no commune could be placed firmly into one or other category, not least because they were dynamic groups, always exploring new possibilities.

The two models varied in how finances (both income and capital) were handled, in how children were reared, in the degree of emotional commitment to the household as a whole, and in gender roles. Communalist ideals did not prevent disputes, which could not always be successfully resolved within the communal framework. Money was always a potential problem, as some members brought in more capital than others, and some more income. The contradiction between the ideal of sharing and the need for privacy, and the demands of sheer physical hard work also created strain. And, while it may be possible to be self-sufficient in food, self-sufficiency in education and health are more difficult.

There were also potential problems between the generations. At what age should children acquire the same domestic, decision-making, financial and sexual rights as their parents? Can children develop their identity without leaving the commune? At the other end of the age scale, few modern communes have yet had to face the problems of an ageing membership, who may become infirm and dependent.

By the early eighties the evangelistic aspect of communes had faded and today they attract less attention. Nevertheless, many supporters of the Green movement see communes as the ideal setting in which to establish decentralised communities and organic farms, and there are perhaps 15 to 20 communes in Britain today, and some hundreds, many with a New Age emphasis, in the U.S. Probably the largest commune in Europe is in Denmark, where 150 people live on a 600-acre estate.

If communalism is seen as a spectrum of values rather than a fixed ideology, then today's housing co-operatives may be placed at the 'soft' end of that spectrum. There is a pleasant irony in the government's support for an activity whose rationale is based on the same collectivist values as those of the Diggers, Robert Owen and, rather more remotely, the tepee people.

10 FEBRUARY 1989

Discussion Topic

What other ways of living have communalist aspects?

FURTHER READING

Abrams, P. and McCulloch, A. (1976) *Communes, Sociology and Society* (CUP).

Oved, Y. (1988) *Two Hundred Years of American Communes* (Transaction Books).

36

Whose Side are You On?

Do Sociologists Condone Crime?

Sociology has, from its earliest years, been the target of criticism from politicians and other people in positions of power. There is little sign of this letting up. But it is in the very nature of good sociology to attract criticism, and it would be a sad day for the discipline if it found itself in harmony with the establishment, or even with itself.

One criticism from outside sociology focuses on the attention that it has paid to deviant behaviour, and argues that sociology sympathises with deviants, criminals, hooligans, even terrorists. A recent example came from Kenneth Baker in November 1989. 'The handmaidens of this revolution were those social scientists and counter-culture prophets who so eagerly propagated excuses for the inexcusable'. By 'revolution' he meant the changes in moral values that he believed had taken place in the 1960s.

A quick scan of the titles of research studies readily confirms that sociology has, since the 1930s, paid a lot of attention to deviant and criminal groups in society and to those whose behaviour is offensive to the majority or to a powerful or vociferous minority. However, there have been two main styles of such research, attracting different kinds of criticism.

Until the 1960s, research into deviant behaviour was dominated, like most sociology, by a search for its causes in objective external factors that exerted pressure on the individual. This style of research, modelled on the methods of the natural sciences, also dominated psychology. The underlying assumption was that deviants and criminals were different from ordinary people and that the cause of this difference lay in some factor or combination of factors which could be identified.

Variations in level of intelligence, chromosomal structure, bodily physique, social class, childhood socialisation, opportunity structures and subcultural context were all identified at one time or another as the

'X' factor which caused, even determined, deviant behaviour.

In so far as such factors are seen to be outside the control of the individual, it is implied that people are no more responsible for their actions than they are for the colour of their eyes. Such a view, found also in determinist versions of Marxism, seems to suggest that people are helpless puppets, unable to resist social, structural and historical pressures any more than leaves can resist falling from the trees in autumn.

It is these determinist explanations of human behaviour that Mr Baker referred to when he said, 'Social scientists tended to argue that behavioural patterns were only the products of social, political and economic factors', and 'To reduce people to mere flotsam and jetsam, buffeted by the tides of society and fashion, is to deny that there can be such a thing as individual identity and therefore individual responsibility'. He quoted from *West Side Story* which, as early as the 1950s, had attacked the determinist approach when the street gang sing 'Hey, I'm depraved on account I'm deprived'.

In the 1960s, however, there was a strong reaction among sociologists against such over-determinism. They began to place more emphasis on the fact that people are conscious, thinking beings who choose how to behave in the light of their view of the world and their interpretation of the situations in which they find themselves. The research techniques developed by the Chicago school of sociology in the 1930s became more widely used. They involved talking directly to deviants and criminals, often in an unstructured interview and usually as part of an ethnography based on participant observation.

Researchers got to know and even to befriend their subjects, with the intention of 'getting inside their heads' and describing their social world from their point of view. This approach has its origins in Weber's notion of *verstehen,* the interpretive understanding of behaviour. It starts from the assumption that people behave rationally and in ways that make sense from their point of view. To discuss football hooligans as 'mindless' is to ensure no understanding of their actions is attempted.

The problem with this approach is that it lays researchers open to the charge that they sympathise with the people they are studying. In some cases this may be true, as when Goffman's *Asylums* revealed what life is like in mental hospitals from the patients' perspective. Howard Becker, in answering the question 'Whose Side Are We On?', says that the issue is not whether to take sides, since this is unavoidable, but whose side to take. He says that he is on the side of the underdogs, because they have the right to be heard, and researchers can ensure that right.

But this does not mean that sociology sympathises with the drug-dealer, the con-man, the hooligan or the violent robber. To describe, to appreciate and to explain is not the same as to justify or to condone. It is possible to understand why people behave as they do and at the same time to condemn that behaviour. The distinction is between 'empathy' and 'sympathy' and social workers make it all the time.

The question of the balance between individual and society, between choice and constraint, and between voluntarism and determinism, is at the heart of the discipline of sociology. The more determinist our explanations of human behaviour, the less moral responsibility accrues to individuals. The more we emphasise freedom of choice and play down the social structure, the more responsibility we place on the individual.

The debate about whether sociology can be value-free is complex, but sociologists should not allow their moral judgement about a social phenomenon to affect the truthfulness of their research reports. Some people behave in ways which range from the mildly irritating to the completely unacceptable, but this should not mean that we do not listen to and report on their accounts. What sociologists are opposed to is ignorance and prejudice, and knowledge is the enemy of these and the prerequisite of rational action.

As the Higginson Report on 'A' levels (1988) put it: 'A free society depends for its strength on the ability of individual members to make sense of their surroundings and think for themselves'. They cannot do this if the only accounts available are those of the law-abiding and the powerful.

17TH FEBRUARY 1989

Discussion Topic

In what circumstances, if any, can people be regarded as not responsible for their actions?

37

Sick as a Parrot

Industrialism and Disease

Salmonella in eggs and poultry; listeria in soft cheeses; danger from unpasteurised milk; outbreaks of legionnaires' disease in London and in the West Midlands: for the medical authorities, the food industry and the politicians 1989 was a bad year.

The government, in particular, finds itself in difficulty. The trend, in recent years, has been to place the responsibility for an individual's health on their own shoulders, through campaigns against smoking, and for healthier eating, more exercise and safe sex. But the source of the latest health hazards is quite clearly outside the control of the individual victim, and action by the state is essential if the spread of disease is to be controlled. This goes against the ideological grain.

But these hazards are not just environmental; they are also specifically industrial. The bacterium which causes legionnaires' disease is found in modern water supplies and air-conditioning systems in urban areas. The salmonella bacterium has been around a long time, but the current concern is with its presence in eggs laid by battery hens on 'factory farms'; listeria has been traced to precooked manufactured foods.

The historical relationship between industrialisation and changing patterns of health and disease is well documented. It can be thought of almost as a profit and loss account, with some diseases becoming less dangerous or being virtually eliminated, while others have become more virulent or more widespread. In Britain from 1830 the death rate fell steadily for all ages and both sexes. This decline and the resulting increase in expectation of life at birth (from about 40 to about 70) is directly associated with a steady decline in fatal infections, of which tuberculosis (TB) was one of the most common.

Other infections, such as measles and whooping cough, are not uncommon but, since the 1930s, deaths from them at any age have become rare. Today, over 60 per cent of all deaths of young men around the age of 20 are caused through accidents or violence. Of these, accidents are much the more significant. (Although the spread of Aids is likely to change this picture in the next few years.) Among middle-aged and elderly men, circulatory diseases are the main cause of death.

In women, the patterns are not clear. Accidents are less significant among young women than young men, but fatal cancers are more common in middle-aged women than in men.

These changes can be characterised as a move from the diseases of poverty to the diseases of affluence. Whereas the poor used frequently to die from infections to which their undernourished bodies had little resistance, in today's much wealthier society people of all classes die of over-eating and under-exercising, and smoking and drinking too much.

There are also various degenerative conditions, not all of them fatal, which are found more commonly in industrial societies with high life expectancy. These include osteoarthritis, arterio-sclerosis and Alzheimer's disease, which typically develop as the organs of the body wear out, though all are aggravated by environmental conditions. These conditions were known to our ancestors, but their prevalence in the population was less, largely because most people did not live long enough for the conditions to develop. In a sense, fatal infections have been virtually eliminated only to create the space for the degenerative conditions to take over as major causes of death. Nevertheless, it is undeniable that economic development dramatically improves people's health.

These changes have taken place not only in an industrial context but also, as Marxists point out, in a capitalist one. Some critics argue that the pursuit of profit generates particular health hazards. In the case of food products, efforts to reduce costs and to compete successfully in the market result in intensive production of meat, milk and eggs in unnatural and hazardous conditions. The production of cereal crops at a competitive price can only be achieved, it is argued, with the help of pesticides to maximise yield per acre. Distribution methods which involve long periods of time between production and consumption require the extensive use of preservatives which may be harmful to health.

Most people have no alternative to obtaining their food from the mass producers who themselves, in a capitalist and profit-oriented economy, have no alternative but to maximise their profit margins, even if this means increased health risks. Producers and distributors are subject to the forces of capitalism just as much as consumers are.

Industrial capitalism also creates health risks in both the working and the wider environment, with atmospheric and noise pollution in and from factories, and the dangers on construction sites and on the roads. The alienation of workers under capitalism is also a health hazard, as stress increases vulnerability to both physical and mental illness.

The problem with this argument is to separate those health risks which are the result of industrialisation generally from those which are the result of its capitalist form. The Marxist argument is that, while many hazards are an inevitable result of industrial processes, it is a matter of choice as to what is manufactured and marketed and how much is spent on creating and enforcing preventive and safety measures. Where profit takes precedence over human welfare, the hazards of industrialism will be greater. To resolve this question would require a controlled comparison between capitalist industrial societies and socialist industrial societies at similar stages of economic development. Since these do not exist, the comparison cannot be made.

Where comparisons have been made between the UK and the countries of Eastern Europe, the evidence does not support a claim that health hazards are any less there.

Perhaps what has taken a knock from recent events is not so much capitalism as the cult of the expert. 'The authorities' have for so long belittled the arguments of the Greens and organic farmers that the need to warn us of danger in a soft-boiled egg is a heavy blow to their credibility.

3 MARCH 1989

Discussion Topic

How do the past and future patterns of the spread of the Aids virus differ from those described in this article?

FURTHER READING

Aggleton, P (1990) *Health* (Routledge).

38

All the World's a Stage

Impression-management in Everyday Life

One of the most obvious things about the Bruno/Tyson world heavy-weight boxing match in 1989 was the theatricality of the whole affair. With a fanfare of trumpets and a flourishing of spotlights, the two protagonists made their entrances into the arena, paraded round the ring and stared at each other as the script required them to do. We even had Tyson in the black shorts of the bad guy and Bruno in the gold lamé-collared dressing-gown of the gentleman. They knew what was expected of them and had rehearsed, at least in imagination, how they would behave.

Erving Goffman, in his dramaturgical model of social life, argues that most, even all, social interaction is like a theatrical performance. In *The Presentation of Self in Everyday Life* he considers

'The way in which the individual in ordinary work situations presents himself and his activity to others, the ways in which he guides and controls the impression they form of him, and the kinds of things he may and may not do while sustaining his performance before them.'

Goffman is aware that the analogy is not perfect. The theatre is make-believe whereas life is real. On stage, actors are portraying char-acters to each other and in front of an audience as third party, whereas in real life people, whom Goffman still calls 'actors', are also each other's audience. In the theatre, the actors are repeating a script and acting out roles, whereas in real life they are, to a much greater extent, improvising the script and creating roles as they go along, though many exchanges are highly ritualised and predictable.

But the analogy holds in many everyday contexts. At job interviews, for example, applicants will take pains over how they present them-selves through their clothing, their demeanour and their speech. In George Mead's terms, they 'take the attitude of the other', trying to see themselves from the potential employer's standpoint and modifying their behaviour to make the desired impression. Such 'impression-management' is also routinely practised by students in relation to teachers and vice versa.

Research has shown, too, how people prepare themselves for a consultation with their doctor by going over the coming conversation in their heads, working out the form of words that will best convey the impression they want to give.

But is all of social life so much play-acting? Goffman argues that it is, though he makes a distinction between 'cynical' performances and sincere ones. The former are where there is a clear gap, of which the actor is aware, between the public performance and the private thoughts, and the latter is where this gap is slight or non-existent. Goffman is not saying that the cynical performance is morally wrong; it is an essential part of social life. Similarly, the sincere performance is no less a performance just because it is genuine.

In his book, Goffman describes the way in which actors work in 'teams', co-operating with each other and feeding each other lines in order to give a third party the desired impression. Policemen, and even teachers, are particularly adept at this, conveying a certainty which they do not really feel.

Goffman also describes the setting and the props which people use to convey their efficiency (e.g. a Filofax), or their status (the office-worker's suit or the managing director's desk), or how busy they are (a conspicuous diary is a favourite prop of social workers calling on clients in their homes). Uniforms are a valuable prop, conveying the wearer's membership of a particular group, and often their rank. They can also be used to symbolise lack of status, as with prison uniforms. Sometimes, actors will deliberately deny their uniform in order to distance themselves from others who wear it. The vicar who wears jeans and a T-shirt is saying 'I'm not like other vicars'.

Goffman also describes how people move between the 'front-region' and the 'back-region' of social settings. 'Front-region' is where the presentation takes place and where the desired impression is most carefully managed. 'Back-region' or 'back-stage' is private, where only insiders are allowed and where a very different version of reality is enacted. Anyone who has worked as a waiter in a smart restaurant will know how the behaviour, attitude and style of the staff in the dining area (front-stage) is transformed when the swing-doors into the kitchen (back-stage) close behind you. The same thing happens when teachers go into the staff-room. That is why pupils are not allowed in, and why they often try to get a quick look before the door closes.

Looking at social life in this way can provide valuable insights into people's behaviour, and is often used when training professionals, both to enable them to convey the desired impression and to bring home to them the impression they are making, whether they are aware of it or not. But there still remains the question of how far such daily perform-ances are deliberate and self-conscious and how far they 'just happen'.

The most skilled and self-conscious impression-managers in everyday life are confidence tricksters, whose stock-in-trade is their ability to project an image and a conviction which deceives their victim. But are ordinary people so manipulative? Is there no spontaneous interaction, where people are just themselves? Frank Bruno certainly lost the ability to manage the impression he was making, and was kept back-stage (off-camera) until he was capable of delivering his next set of lines, to cues provided by Harry Carpenter.

Goffman's detailed observation and analysis of everyday life has been rejected by some sociologists who argue that it fails to take account of wider social structures and the importance of power. In fact, while he pays little attention to the structures of power, Goffman has written extensively about the use and abuse of power in personal relationships. It is impossible to read his work without occasionally recognising oneself in his descriptions, though only Tyson and Bruno could tell us how much of their pre-fight performance was cynical and how much was sincere.

10 MARCH 1989

Discussion Topic

How far can these ideas be applied to interaction between parents and their adolescent children?

FURTHER READING

Goffman, E. (1959/71) *The Presentation of Self in Everyday Life* (Penguin).

39

Body and Soul

How Religions are Organised

March 17 is the first day of Ramadan, the ninth month in the Muslim calendar, and in which the prophet Muhammad received his first revelations. During Ramadan, devout Muslims are commanded to fast from dawn to sunset for the whole month.

How many people in Britain can be expected to follow this command? *Social Trends 1989* estimates that there are about 900,000 adult Muslims in the United Kingdom, making them the third largest religious group after Protestants (4,868,000) and Roman Catholics (2,059,000), having more than doubled their numbers since 1975. *Britain: an Official Handbook* estimates a total of 1,500,000 Muslims in Britain, including a growing community who are British-born and an increasing number of converts. But even if the total figure could be accurately established, how could we find out how many obeyed the command to fast?

To be a member of a religious organisation is not necessarily to accept all its teachings or to obey all its commands. Even in Iran, where the religious leaders are also the political leaders, it is estimated that only 10 per cent of the population of 40 million are fundamentalist Muslims.

Religious organisations in Britain come in all sizes, and range from the private and secretive to the conspicuously public and evangelical. All are in a continuous state of change, both as individual organisations and in terms of relative importance in the overall religious life of this country.

Until recently, the Muslim community in Britain attracted relatively little media attention, except where it overlapped with the mainly hostile and sometimes covertly racist coverage of Iran and Ayatollah Khomeini, but the controversy over Salman Rushdie's *The Satanic Verses* has changed that.

To help make sense of the variety of religious organisations, sociologists have traditionally used three ideal types: church, sect and denomination. A 'church' is a large formal religious organisation with a paid hierarchy of officials based on a priesthood. It claims to minister

117

to all members of a society and to all social strata. It has a high proportion of middle- and upper-class members and is integrated with and supports the social and economic order of society, having a close relationship with the state. It is intolerant of other religious beliefs and claims a monopoly of the truth, sometimes promoting this truth through missionary work. Membership of a church is conferred by birth. An example of a church might be the Roman Catholic Church in Eire (or in Italy in the past), or Islam in Iran or Saudi Arabia today.

A denomination is smaller than a church, but also has a bureaucratic and hierarchical organisation. It keeps itself detached from the state and tolerates and co-operates with other religious organisations. Though it recruits from all social classes, the lower classes are over-represented among its members. A denomination generally accepts or at least compromises with the norms and values of society, though there may be some degree of evangelism.

In terms of this model, the contemporary Church of England is more a denomination than a church. Though it still has close formal links with the established social and political order, it finds itself increasingly at odds with the government of the day, it tolerates other religions, and it has adapted its moral guidance in various respects.

The classical model of a sect is of a small group with egalitarian relationships and no formal hierarchy or bureaucracy. Its leadership is often charismatic, especially in the early days of the sect's existence. Its members are often drawn from the lower classes, the poor and the deprived. They believe themselves to be the elect, the chosen ones. The sect rejects the values of the wider society and the beliefs of other religious groups, claiming a monopoly of the truth. A sect is exclusive, only accepting as members those who meet its standards of suitability. It may be actively evangelical, seeking to increase its membership through conversions. A sect exercises close control over its members' lives and requires obedience and intense commitment from them. Sects often emerge as the result of a split within a church or a denomination, usually on doctrinal grounds. The Methodists originated in this way. In the classical model, sects are often unstable and short-lived.

Sociologists have been particularly fascinated by sects, partly because their very secretiveness and marginality is a research challenge, but also because many have flourished in recent years, against the supposed trend towards secularisation. Groups like the Unification Church (the Moonies), the Children of God and Hare Krishna have increased all over the world, and are not limited in their membership to the deprived. Studies of these groups have, however, revealed many inadequacies in the traditional typology outlined in this article, and the term 'New Religious Movement' (NRM) has become widely used. This term has, in its turn, been refined (Beckford, 1985).

Despite its faults, the classical typology does help in analysing changing patterns of religious organisation and in comparing the role of a particular religious group in different societies at the same time. Thus the Baptists, once a breakaway sect, are now an established denomination, which has had its own share of sectarian conflict over the years. The Mormons, essentially sectarian in the UK, are more church-like in Salt Lake City, Utah. The Roman Catholic Church in South America, far from being aligned with the ruling powers, now espouses 'liberation theology' and has links with revolutionary Marxism.

Britain's Muslims are too numerous to be called a sect, they are not a church, and the reaction to *The Satanic Verses* suggests an intolerance which is not associated with denominations. But do all British Muslims share the views of the book-burners? A proper analysis would find a range of views, rather than the stereotyped fanaticism portrayed by the popular press.

7 APRIL 1989

Discussion Topic

How important is Christianity in British social and political life today?

FURTHER READING

Beckford, J.A. (1985) 'Religious Organisations', in Hammond, P., *The Sacred in a Post-secular Age* (University of California Press).

40

Citizens' Rights

The Concept of Citizenship

As soon as the exam season is over, the summer holidays begin, and thoughts may turn to foreign travel. For that a passport is needed, as evidence of the holder's British (or other) citizenship and right to return to the UK from abroad. A British citizen is entitled to live, move and work freely within the territories known as 'Great Britain and Northern Ireland' and to enjoy the benefits of 'membership' of the British state. These include the right to vote, to join political parties and other political organisations, to stand for election, to equality before the law, to freedom of speech and from wrongful imprisonment within Britain.

Citizens also have duties to the state. For example, they must pay taxes levied by the state, whether locally or nationally; they must obey the laws of the state; and they are liable to service in the state's military organisations.

The significance of citizenship is underlined when you realise that, while in another country, you are a visitor, or, technically, an 'alien'. You may be accorded certain facilities, such as hiring a car or even earning a living, but you have not the same formal rights as a citizen and, if you fall foul of a foreign government, you may be 'deported'.

The role of citizen is not related to family background, class or wealth. At least, that has been the theory of citizenship until recently. However, in *New Statesman* (29 April 1988) Douglas Hurd, the Home Secretary, introduced the notion of 'responsible and active citizenship', and accused the left of being 'stuck with the bureaucratic definition of citizenship as something to which we are compelled by the state'.

It appears that Mr Hurd wishes to part company with the idea of the citizen as a 'member of the state' and to emphasise the notion of 'active citizens', who will give their time voluntarily to help the community. Presumably this means that those who are homeless, infirm, unemployed, poor or discriminated against will be deprived of full 'state membership' because they are unlikely to have the time or, more particularly, the inclination to help the community. They will be, literally, second-class citizens.

The modern concept of citizenship emerged during the French Re-volution when the 'citoyen' was seen as an individual who was entitled to political rights and protection from enemies in return for loyalty to the nation-state. All French people would be equal before the law. In Britain, the development of full equality of citizenship was a longer process. In 1947 the English sociologist T.H. Marshall wrote an influ-ential essay in which he suggested that citizenship had three com-ponents – civil, political and social – which developed over different periods of history.

Civil citizenship, which developed in England roughly between 1688 and 1832, involved the right to equal protection under the law and freedom of speech and thought. For instance, the principle of *habeas corpus* ensured freedom from arbitrary imprisonment, while freedom of speech and thought was encouraged by the repeal of laws censoring the press.

Political citizenship emerged from 1832 onwards with the reform of Parliament and the extension of voting rights, first at national level and then in local government. The formation of mass political parties further strengthened political citizenship.

Social citizenship, according to Marshall, dated particularly from 1946 with the creation of the welfare state based on the principle of insurance and universality of benefit; everyone contributed and every-one benefited. In addition a free and universal education system would ensure access to knowledge for everyone, not just an educated elite.

Marshall argued that, although the civil component of citizenship gave equal rights to all individuals it did not give individuals the ability to exercise those rights. Poverty and ignorance rendered civil rights largely theoretical. Marshall was more hopeful that political rights would give the working class greater power, but no working-class government has held power for very long in Britain.

For Marshall in 1947, the great breakthrough to equality of citizen-ship had come with free education and the establishment of a social security net. Although he thought that some inequality might always be necessary, he also felt that the emergence of 'social' citizenship would entitle the masses to sufficient economic security to enable them to enjoy the status of citizen equally with the middle and upper classes.

Marshall was a reformist. He thought that a genuine citizenship could be created within the framework of the capitalist state. Marxists see it differently. For them, citizenship is part of that hegemonic proc-ess in which the masses learn their rights and duties as citizens, in terms set by the dominant ideology. So long as they feel that they are citizens, they feel free and do not threaten the capitalist, social and economic order. In this view, citizenship is a disguise which hides continuing inequalities of wealth and power.

Nevertheless, it seems that some Conservatives are not happy with a concept of citizenship which requires the state to ensure a minimum economic status for all citizens by creating a complex bureaucracy to interfere with the 'natural' workings of the market. This is what Douglas Hurd means by a 'bureaucratic' definition of citizenship. To Conservatives it smacks of regimentation and collectivism. But it is not necessary to be a Marxist to see that, without the rights guaranteed by the welfare state, gross inequalities of income, wealth and status make a mockery of the other rights of citizenship.

The government has advanced the idea of the 'active citizen' who voluntarily helps others and takes part in civic affairs. Are there then to be two classes of citizen, the one active, the other passive? If so, does this differ from the definition of citizenship based on equality? Is it a return to citizenship based on wealth and privilege? The year 1989 is the 200th anniversary of the French Revolution; will citizens have to storm the Bastille again?

21 APRIL 1989

Discussion Topic

To what extent are citizenship rights undermined by social and economic equality?

FURTHER READING

Marshall, T.H. (1963) 'Citizenship and Social Class', in *Sociology at the Crossroads* (Heinemann), reprinted in Held, D. (1983) *States and Societies* (Martin Robertson).

41

In the Dock

Working-class Communities

The dockers' 1989 decision to strike is not regarded as a serious threat to the national economy. There was a time when it would have been. For example, extended unofficial strike action in 1967, when Harold Wilson's Labour government was in power, contributed to the decision to devalue the pound by 14 per cent.

It is a measure of the decline in the industrial muscle of dock-workers that their threat of action, in response to government proposals to scrap the National Dock Scheme, has produced little response.

In 1947, when the scheme was introduced, there were 79,000 registered dockers. Today, there are 9400 (*The Independent*, 11 April 1989). In this massive reduction in numbers lies the obvious cause of the decline of dockers' industrial strength. The reduction is the result of changing practices in the transport of goods (more use of lorries and roll-on roll-off ferries) and of changes in cargo-handling techniques (such as containerisation). In addition, changing patterns of trade among UK ports has meant the virtual extinction of the London docks and much-reduced activity in Liverpool as work has been transferred to non-scheme ports on the East Coast.

These changes have not only affected the industrial strength of dockers, but have also transformed the dockland communities, which were traditionally regarded as strongholds of working-class solidarity. The concept of an 'occupational community' was developed in the 1950s and 1960s. Though the concept is now used rather differently (Salaman, 1986), in its original form it referred to communities in the fullest sense: that is, to a physical locality with a set of social relationships (not necessarily harmonious) which take place wholly or mainly within that locality, and whose members have a sense of shared identity, often involving strong class consciousness and a sense of Them-and-Us.

Ethnographic studies were carried out of such working-class occupational communities as the Liverpool docks (1954) and of 'Ashton', the coal-mining town (in fact, Featherstone) described in the classic study *Coal is Our Life* by Dennis, Henriques and Slaughter (1956). It described a community in which the nature of the men's work was the overwhelming influence on marriage and family life, on attitudes to education, on leisure pursuits and friendship patterns, on class consciousness, on religious activity (usually Nonconformist), on political allegiances (which were collectivist), and on every aspect of social life.

A similar study was Tunstall's *The Fishermen* (1962) which described the way of life of the trawlermen of Hull and the impact of their work on their relationships with each other and on their lives ashore. The shared characteristic of these occupational communities was a pattern of hard manual work in an isolated area. A similar lifestyle is described in *The North Wales Quarrymen 1874–1922* by Merfyn Jones (1982).

An ideal-typical account of the traditional male worker, based on some of these studies, appeared in an influential article by Lockwood in 1966. In the 1970s and 1980s, however, there has been some debate about whether these communities ever existed as described. Dennis Warwick, for example, went back to Featherstone in the early eighties and was told by some informants, now 30 years older, that Dennis and his colleagues had looked for and found stereotypes that supported their own preconceptions. There was, it is suggested, more division within the communities than the researchers recognised.

Though *Family and Kinship in East London* (Young and Willmott, 1957) emphasises the high status of dockers in the East End, there was no substantial study of dockers between the 1954 study in Liverpool and Stephen Hill's *The Dockers* (1976). Hill had two aims in this book. The first was to give an account of the social and industrial behaviour and attitudes of London dock workers, 'a group of men who have often been maligned by the press and misunderstood by sociology', and the second was to define the position of dock workers in the class structure.

His description of work in the docks shows how the changes in working practices described above had already begun to take effect. He found that, even as early as 1969–71 when he did his research, the conventional stereotype of dockers as traditional workers was no longer appropriate, even assuming it had ever been correct. Just as Goldthorpe and Lockwood in the *Affluent Worker* studies (1968) found that highly-paid manual workers were not following traditional working-class lifestyles, though certainly not adopting those of the middle class, so Hill found little evidence of traditional working-class consciousness among the dockers.

Rebuilding in the East End, the movement of populations out into the suburbs and the New Towns, the greater ease of commuting, the decline in numbers and changes in the attitudes and behaviour of dock-workers: all these

'Suggest that most aspects of working-class traditionalism . . . have long since disappeared in this occupation. Patterns of sociability and labour recruitment do reflect the existence of a kind of occupational community, though this is neither very concentrated geographically nor are people's lives very influenced by it . . . the characteristic home-life is family-centred and private. Some gregariousness is evident but it falls far short of what is regarded as traditional working-class behaviour.'

The 1984–5 miners' strike was portrayed by the NUM as a last, and in the event unsuccessful, attempt by a sector of the traditional working class to defend their jobs and their communities. In the end, it became apparent that there was greater solidarity in some communities than in others. It may be that the extent of working-class solidarity based on occupational communities has always been overestimated. This, coupled with the effects of economic change, has prompted a reconsideration of the links between work, community, class and political allegiance.

26 MAY 1989

Discussion Topic

What other jobs might generate 'occupational communities'?

FURTHER READING

Bulmer, M. (1975) *Working Class Images of Society* (RKP).
Salaman, G. (1986) *Working* (Tavistock).

42

Accidents can Happen

Safety at Work

The sinking of the *Herald of Free Enterprise*, the Piper Alpha oil-rig disaster, the King's Cross fire, the M1 plane crash, the train crashes at Purley, Glasgow and Clapham, and the disaster at Hillsborough – events like these, caused by accident or neglect rather than by sabotage – have been all too frequent in the last few years. They are always followed by demands for an inquiry into causes and for the identification of anyone responsible for the failure of health and safety precautions.

The question of responsibility is not just a moral one. The existence of regulations and laws governing safety at work or in public places means that this is an area where the sociologies of health, of the state, of crime and of the media meet and overlap. A dramatic illustration of this is the inquest jury's verdict of unlawful killing on 187 of the people who died in the *Herald of Free Enterprise*.

The sociology of the mass media draws our attention to the news values that influence the selection of stories for coverage. All these events are newsworthy in that they are highly visible, they are unusual, they can be graphically presented, they are of brief duration, and they have a strong focus of 'human interest' (Chibnall, 1977).

Chibnall contrasts this with the relatively slight media attention given to the routine injuries and violence that are the result of industrial pollution, unsafe working conditions or practices, or the damage caused by the mental stress of repetitive work. Where such conditions are the result of breaches of the law, the media may be seen as systematically under-reporting offences committed by powerful people and agencies.

Laws governing health and safety are unusual in that they are usually concerned with regulating the activities of powerful people such as employers, proprietors and managers. This contrasts with the traditional focus of law enforcement and of criminology – the working-class male. Recent criticism of conventional criminology has argued that the inverse relationship between social class and crime – as one goes up, the other goes down – is partly a consequence of the fact that there are more laws governing the working class. But how does this tally with the existence of health and safety laws which target the powerful?

Factory legislation stems from the 19th century. Some employers at that time did accept that such laws might be in their long-term interests – legitimising the social order, and protecting their workforce, especially as labour became more skilled. However, opposition from factory owners to this state intervention was widespread and vigorous.

Such opposition is still apparent today when, despite considerable improvements in working conditions, there were still 7000 deaths or serious injuries in industry and construction in 1984, and the trend was upward (*Guardian*, 11 February 1986). The same article referred to Trade Secretary Lord Young's sympathetic response to the fact that 'some businessmen still complain to me that they are unhappy about the weight of work which health and safety legislation puts upon them'.

As far as prosecutions are concerned, this 'burden' on industry would not seem to be a problem. One study in the 1960s involved a survey of 200 randomly selected companies in the south east, using files from the Chief Inspector of Factories. This identified 3800 offences, half of which concerned inadequately guarded machinery or insufficient precautions against fire. There were ten prosecutions arising from these offences (Carson, 1970). Carson says that the Inspectorate's emphasis was on seeing prosecution as a means to an end (promoting safety), rather than as an end in itself (punishing wrong-doing), and so the prosecution rate is not evidence of conscious class bias in law enforcement.

Another analysis of this issue is provided by Steven Box (1987). Exploring the possible links between economic recession and crime, he argues that too much attention has been given to the possible growth of working-class crime, such as by the unemployed, during these economic downturns. He argues that recession is just as likely to cause an increase in corporate crime as profit margins are squeezed.

Adapting a theory of the causes of crime first developed by Robert Merton, Box suggests that, as corporate goals become harder to achieve legitimately, innovation may occur. Such innovation may include avoidance or evasion of the law through selling untested products, or less rigorous quality control and safety checks, or price-fixing, and so on. He refers to one piece of American research from the early 1970s which shows a correlation between factors such as company profitability and performance and rates of illegal activities.

Not only does recession increase the likelihood of corporate crime but also, he argues, government will often view the plight of companies sympathetically. Because of this, an atmosphere of deregulation may develop so that campaigning for revision of the law, as well as its evasion, becomes a business strategy. It may be argued that the same pressures exist in times of rapid economic growth.

Possible evidence of weaker enforcement of the law could be provided by the fall in the number of factory inspectors from 951 in 1979 to 792 in 1988 (*Guardian*, 16 November 1988) and the new employment legislation, which abolishes restrictions on the number of hours that 16–18-year-olds can work. The latter is interesting given that, from 1984 to 1988, the rate of major accidents for young people on Youth Training Schemes rose from 63 to 156 per 100,000 trainees. (*This Week*, 9 March 1989).

It appears that big and unusual accidents make more news but cause fewer deaths and injuries than minor but common accidents. But most accidents, large or small, are seldom only the result of bad luck.

2 JUNE 1989

Discussion Topic

Should employers who break the law and cause injuries to employees be dealt with as severely as other violent offenders?

FURTHER READING

Box, S. (1987) *Recession, Crime and Punishment* (Macmillan).

Carson, W.G. (1970) 'White Collar Crime and the Enforcement of Factory Legislation', *Brit. J. of Crimin.* 10.

Chibnall, S. (1977) *Law and Order News* (Tavistock).

43

The Green Light

The Rise of the Greens

In the county council elections on 5 May 1989 the Green Party polled 8.7 per cent of the vote in the 209 seats it contested, and one Green councillor was elected in the Isle of Wight. In the elections for the European parliament, the Greens had a candidate in every constituency.

But Britain still trails the rest of Europe on green politics, although the environment is now firmly on the political agenda. Evidence can be found in the number of recent front-page news stories about the environment, and in the number of parliamentary debates on green issues.

But why this increased prominence for the environment? The most obvious answer is that environmental threats have increased and are more severe than was the case a few years ago. This is in a sense true, but it is not the most convincing explanation. Several aspects of the environmental crisis were well-documented in a number of widely-read books published around 1970. Among the most famous are *The Limits to Growth* (Donella H. Meadows *et al.*), *A Blueprint for Survival* (Edward Goldsmith and *The Ecologist* team) and *Silent Spring* (Rachel Carson). The significant point is that it is not so much the objective conditions of the environmental crisis that have changed, but rather our perception of them. Pressure groups like Friends of the Earth and Greenpeace have been particularly effective in pushing environmental issues to the forefront of public debate.

But it was not only the politicians who ignored environmental problems. For the most part they were also ignored by social scientists, the exception being a study by the American political scientist Matthew A. Crenson, entitled *The Unpolitics of Air Pollution: a Study of Non-decision-making in the Cities* (1971).

Crenson examined the political processes in two similar, and equally polluted, American cities and asked why one of the cities passed clean air legislation and the other did not. He concluded that pollution was not even defined as a political issue in one city because the might of the polluters ensured it was kept off the political agenda. The lesson he drew from this study is that the sources of political neglect are themselves highly political and that political power is most effective when it is invisible. Despite this early study, only now are environmental politics being considered in social science textbooks, such as *Contemporary British Politics* by Coxall and Robins (1989) and *Sociology* by Giddens (1989).

Significantly, however, the emergence of environmental issues into the political arena has ensured the growth of Green political parties. When the first Green MP was elected in Switzerland in 1979 it was regarded as rather a freak event, but in 1981 nine Green MPs were elected in Belgium and, when 28 members of the West German Green Party, *Die Grunen*, were elected to the Bundestag in 1983, even *The Times* declared 'Green revolution marches on Bonn'.

Greens are now represented in the following European parliaments: Austria (eight), Belgium (nine), Finland (four), West Germany (41), Italy (13), Luxembourg (two), Portugal (one), Sweden (20) and Switzerland (nine). Virtually all West European countries have a large number of Greens elected at local government level, and there are eleven Green MPs in the European Parliament.

The British Green Party is still only of marginal significance, however, largely because of the peculiarities of our electoral system which discriminates against smaller parties. It does not mean that there is little interest in environmental matters in Britain. Quite the opposite. The Green Party may have only 8000 members compared to *Die Grunen*'s 43,000, but, because of our particular political system, it has been environmental pressure groups which have had the greatest political significance in Britain.

If we take this into account, we have one of the most flourishing environmental movements in Western Europe. It has been estimated that three million people in Britain belong to environmental groups, a total larger than the combined membership of all the political parties. Recent opinion polls show that environmental problems are now regarded by many people as being the single most urgent political issue.

Environmental pressure groups have raised public awareness and pressured the government into action on issues ranging from clean air, countryside protection and the use of CFC containers, to international problems like the depletion of the ozone layer and global warming due to the greenhouse effect. As a result, all the political parties have been frantically greening themselves in order to reap the benefits of the green vote.

However, over a wide range of environmental issues Britain has one of the worst records in Western Europe. Britain is responsible for a significant proportion of the sulphur emissions that cause acid rain. And, in many European and international forums, Britain consistently sabotages attempts to impose tough environmental legislation. At home too, the government rarely takes a tough line on environmental protection and it fails adequately to enforce the relatively weak controls that do exist.

In addition, the government is sometimes unwilling to comply with environmental directives emanating from the EC. For instance, in many areas of Britain the drinking water breaches EC standards relating to water contamination.

The government's environmental record has been highlighted in a carefully documented report from Friends of the Earth published in 1989. It argues that the government is reluctant to acknowledge the existence of environmental problems, does its best to suppress un-favourable evidence, strenuously challenges any evidence until such tactics prove untenable and, when eventually forced into action, enacts inadequate measures. Even these are often not rigorously implemented.

Nevertheless, it is clear that in Britain, as elsewhere, environmental problems are now politically significant. Governments which ignore them in the coming decade may pay a heavy electoral price.

9 JUNE 1989

Discussion Topic

What environmental issues are becoming important in local politics in your area?

FURTHER READING

Porritt, J. and Winner, D. (1988) *The Coming of the Greens* (Fontana).

Muller-Rommel, F. (ed.) (1989) *New Politics in Western Europe* (Westview Press.)

44

The Good Terrorist

Theories of Terrorism

Terror is a state of mind which can be induced and then exploited by an individual or group wishing to dominate any other individual or group, or even a whole society, in order to promote a sectional interest. It is also used by states as a tool of domestic and of foreign policy.

The Chinese Communist Party under Deng Xiaoping has used terror to suppress the student democratic movement. Thousands are reported to have been killed as students and workers were cleared by the army from Tiananmen Square in Beijing. An historical example is 'The Terror' which followed the French Revolution. Between 1793 and 1794 the Jacobins defended the progress of the revolution by guillotining thousands – not just aristocrats – who were seen as a counter-revolutionary threat.

Since 1945, politically-motivated terrorism, as distinct from a domestic regime of terror, has become more widespread and more international, and is usually associated with factions challenging the authority of states. Wilkinson (1986) defines political terrorism as coercive intimidation, 'the systematic use of murder and destruction and the threat of murder and destruction in order to terrorise individuals, groups, communities or governments into conceding to the terrorists' political demands'. The essential ingredient of terrorism in the age of mass communications is not so much that thousands should be killed as that they should be terrified.

Political terrorism takes various forms. Wilkinson divides these into repressive terrorism, which is used by states to suppress dissenting groups or individuals as in China; sub-revolutionary terrorism, which seeks legal or political change short of revolution (for example, the Animal Liberation Front); and revolutionary terrorism, which seeks substantial political change. This may be broadly ideological, as in the anti-capitalist (especially anti-American) activities of Action Directe in

France or the German Red Brigades, or regional, as in the case of ETA (the Basque independence group in Spain), the Provisional IRA, and the many Palestinian groups.

Pure terrorist violence has certain characteristics which distinguish it from other forms of violence. It is indiscriminate in its victims, some of whom at least must be 'innocent', in the sense that they have no repressive or military role. The bomb in the aircraft which crashed on Lockerbie was indiscriminate, whereas a bomb planted at a military barracks is not. The IRA bomb at the Grand Hotel in Brighton in 1984, intended to kill members of the Cabinet, falls somewhere between these two.

Terrorist violence is arbitrary and unpredictable, whereas violence in war, including guerrilla war, is governed by rules, both formal and informal, many of which are embodied in the Geneva Convention. Terrorists are not constrained, as are conventional military operations, by any moral or legal inhibitions about the cruelty of the weapons they use. Lastly, politically-motivated terrorists will claim that their violence is justified in the furtherance of their goals.

Such a justification is based on the belief that terrorism achieves its objectives. In the short term, this is often the case, and a relatively small group can gain massive publicity, collect a ransom, have prisoners released, or provoke so repressive a reaction from the authorities that others are prompted to support its campaign. In the longer term, however, says Wilkinson, terrorism alone rarely achieves its goals.

Where it has been successful, there have been special circumstances. Thus in Palestine in the 1940s, in Cyprus in the 1950s and in Aden and Algeria in the 1960s, terrorism contributed to the departure of the occupying forces. But in these cases the colonial power was constrained by humanitarian and legal factors from taking action that would effectively have eliminated the terrorists. Many acts of great cruelty were done in the name of law and order in these colonial wars, but there were not mass executions. In addition, there was intercommunal conflict which made a peaceful withdrawal impossible, and the terrorists had substantial support from the indigenous population.

In some circumstances, the effect of terrorist activity has been to harden the resolve of governments, and sometimes of the population at large, not to give in to terrorist demands. This may create a situation where a liberal democratic state passes essentially undemocratic laws in its attempts to defeat the terrorists and retain a monopoly on the legitimate right to use violence to achieve its ends. Individual civil rights are then limited by anti-terrorist legislation. This is the case with the Prevention of Terrorism Act in the UK, whose provisions for the detention of suspects give much more power to the state than do the laws of *habeas corpus* in ordinary criminal cases. The same is true of non-jury 'Diplock Courts' in Northern Ireland.

The use of terrorism for criminal purposes can blur the issue further. Straightforward criminal terrorism, including 'consumer terrorism' (as in the recent case of the contaminated baby-food), is done for financial gain, whereby a ransom is gained for the release of hostages or for the cessation of an activity. The blurring occurs where the money is collected to buy weapons to further a terrorist campaign, as with the bank robberies carried out by the IRA. The British government's policy of treating Irish terrorists as 'common criminals' reflects their desire to depoliticise terrorism.

The growing internationalism of terrorism is apparent as groups whose goals are internal to one state, such as the Palestine Liberation Organisation, attack targets abroad. States such as Libya and Iran sponsor international terrorism, and many groups supply each other with support, training and weapons and with refuge.

Whereas terrorism was once the concern only of the state whose political system was under attack, it is today a source of diplomatic conflict and can threaten international peace.

16 JUNE 1989

Discussion Topic

Should terrorists be interviewed for TV programmes?

FURTHER READING

Wilkinson, P. (1986) *Terrorism and the Liberal State* (Macmillan).

45
Unnatural Breaks

The History of Holidays

The Spring bank holiday; queues at the passport office; portents of doom from the package tour companies: holidays are here again.

There is nothing new about the idea of holidays, but they have changed dramatically in character in the last two centuries, especially for ordinary people. The aristocracy have been taking foreign holidays since the 17th century (when the word 'tourist' was first used) and the middle classes travelled widely in the 19th century as the railways expanded.

But for the working class the origin of 'holidays' lies in 'holy days', the designated days in the medieval Christian calendar, as many as one in three, when people were supposed to desist from work. The year was made up of periods of intense labour and hardship interspersed with feast days when meat and drink were plentiful, and dancing, sports, drinking and courting took place.

The suffix '-tide', as in Eastertide and Christmastide, means 'feast'. Some of these festival days were combined with a fair, when merchants and traders would assemble, often travelling great distances, to deal in goods and also to buy local produce.

This pattern persisted until the early part of the Industrial Revolution, and indeed into the 19th century in rural areas. However, the teachings of the Puritans in the 17th century and the Methodists in the 18th started a reaction against such festivities (Pilgrim in Bunyan's *Pilgrim's Progress* was exposed to the evils of the flesh at Vanity Fair). They reached a climax in the period between 1780 and 1830. At the same time the ability of people to govern the tempo of their own working lives was under pressure from the demands of changes in the technology of production, which meant that manual employees became controlled by the clock and the factory shift.

Many of the traditional holy days and festivals were suppressed, despite resistance, during the 19th century, as employers required their workers to work long hours with few or no days off. Work and leisure became separated rather than interwoven and 'free time' came to be demanded as a right by organised labour.

The state became involved through the Factory Acts, and the first results of the struggle to win back leisure time for working people came with an act in 1874 which limited the working day to ten hours. This was followed in stages by the granting of the right to holidays and then to paid holidays. This, in its turn, gave rise to the mass leisure industries, so the consumption of goods and services in leisure-time was well established by the time of the First World War. Even so, the distinction between work and leisure was more real for men than for women, whose domestic labour continued long after the factory shift was over.

Some of the traditional fairs were still being held, albeit in a modified form, up to the end of the 19th century. One of the greatest was Bartholomew Fair (on the feast of St Bartholomew) with menageries, pantomimes, card sharps, sword-swallowers and other delights. The tradition of Wakes Week in north-west England still survives, as does Goose Fair in Nottingham and Tor Fair in Glastonbury, though these are now simply large fun-fairs.

From the beginning of the 20th century and through into the 1950s, the pattern of day-trips and outings for working-class people was established. These were the great days of resorts like Blackpool and Clacton, though Scarborough and Brighton had been catering for a wealthier clientele for many years.

The past 25 years have seen the most dramatic growth and changes in the pattern of holiday-making for working people, through a combination of growing affluence and rapid mass transport.

In 1963 (just as the heyday of the holiday camps began to fade) 97 per cent of full-time manual workers received two weeks' paid holiday a year. By 1985, 99 per cent received at least four weeks. In 1971, 41 million holidays away from home were taken (seven million of them abroad) and by 1985 this figure had risen to 49 million (of which 16 million were abroad). In 1987 20 million foreign holidays were taken, 31 per cent of them in Spain, with an additional 75 million holidays being spent in Britain, half of which were for three nights or less. These overall figures conceal, however, that the proportion of people who took no holiday at all, 40 per cent, did not change over this period. Most of the increase is accounted for by the rise to 21 per cent of those taking more than one holiday.

Who takes holidays? And who takes which kind of holiday? In terms of social class, whereas some 20 per cent of classes A and B took no holiday in 1986, this was true of nearly 60 per cent of classes D and E. About 15 per cent of AB classes took three or more holidays, compared to 3 per cent of D and E. In terms of age, over half of adults aged over 65 did not have a holiday in 1987, compared to just over a third of those aged between 25 and 54.

How do people spend holidays, other than as tourists? According to the English Tourist Board, many second and third holidays are activity holidays, ranging from hot-air ballooning and pot-holing to mock battles and 'murder week-ends'.

It is ironic, given the struggles of the 19th century, that one of the fastest growing types of holiday is the working holiday, often organised by a conservation group such as the British Trust for Conservation Volunteers. Similarly, a visit to an out of town DIY hypermarket on any bank holiday shows how many people spend their holiday working in the informal economy.

But the early origins of holidays are still apparent. The dates of Christmas and Easter are still fixed by the religious festivals. The puritan ethic survives in the anger directed at unemployed people holidaying on the 'Costa del Dole', and many people talk of 'deserving' a holiday, rather than taking one as a right.

23 JUNE 1989

Discussion Topic

Many people talk about 'getting away from it all'. But what is 'it'?

FURTHER READING

Deem, R. (1988) *Work, Unemployment and Leisure* (Tavistock).

Thompson, E.P. (1968) *The Making of the English Working Class* (Pelican).

46

Moving Houses

Winners and Losers in the Housing Market

In April 1989, the Salvation Army and Surrey University carried out a survey of people sleeping rough in London, the first since the 19th century. The results will give a snapshot of the current situation, with evidence of recent trends. The fact that the survey was done indicates that the problem of sleeping rough is thought to be on the increase.

Sociologists know, of course, that growing concern about an issue is no proof that the problem is itself expanding. It is widely believed, however, that the growing concern about homelessness is not just a matter of heightened awareness but an indication of real changes in the housing market.

This market is usually analysed by classification into three types of tenure: privately rented, owner-occupied (including mortgaged) and rented from the local authority (council housing). The balance between these has changed dramatically during this century as the following figures show. Privately rented: 1914 – 90 per cent; 1951 – 52 per cent; 1983 – 12 per cent. Owner-occupied: 1914 – 10 per cent; 1951 – 31 per cent; 1983 – 62 per cent. Council housing: 1914 – 0 per cent; 1951 – 17 per cent; 1983 – 26 per cent (Parker and Mirrlees, 1988). This last figure represents a slight decline since 1980 as the Tory government's policy of opposition to council housing began to take effect.

Not only have council house sales risen substantially since the introduction in 1980 of the right to buy but building has effectively ceased. From 1975 to 1979 an average of 120,000 council dwellings were built each year; in 1989/90 the estimated number is 12,000. Recent measures have encouraged the transfer of council tenancies to private landlords or to voluntary housing associations, and have enlarged the latter's role.

There is a correlation between type of tenure and the condition of housing, as well as with the income level of the occupier. There are also significant variations within types of tenure. The privately rented sector has the highest percentage of households lacking a basic amenity such as a bath or an inside lavatory, or with too few bedrooms for the number of occupants.

Nearly all council houses have these minimum requirements, while outright owners are slightly less likely to have them. Such people are often retired and unable to modernise their properties. People with mortgages generally have the highest quality of housing, though those in old inner city areas may be an exception to this. Murie (1983) argues that traditional ways of measuring housing deprivation do not take account of factors like the external environment of the housing.

For example, some will be of very high density, lack adequate health, education or shopping provision in the locality, or may have a poor reputation in the eyes of the police or other local organisations.

While there are some low-income owner-occupiers (especially single parents, the elderly, and the unemployed) and some better-off council tenants, there is still a correlation between income and type of tenure. In 1977, the percentage of householders in each tenure type who were in receipt of supplementary benefit, rent rebate or rate rebate was as follows: council tenants – 40 per cent; private tenants, furnished – 33 per cent; outright owners – 27 per cent; mortgage buyers – 3 per cent (Murie, 1983).

It would be wrong to conclude that the low level of benefit claimants among people with mortgages means that they received no housing subsidy from public funds. Tax relief on mortgages cost £2340 million in 1983/84, about £8 million more than the cost of housing subsidies by local and central government for publicly owned dwellings (Parker and Mirrlees, 1988). The cost of the relief has since doubled. Unlike housing benefit, this is given regardless of income. The spread of home ownership, combined with the worsening of economic circumstances for many householders in the 1980s, has contributed to growing money problems for mortgage-holders. In 1988 the building societies repossessed 20,000 homes because of mortgage arrears, a 900 per cent increase on 1979 (*Guardian*, 31 May 1989).

With the decline of the privately rented sector, more affluent tenants have moved into owner-occupation and poorer ones into council accommodation. As the better-off tenants increasingly buy higher-quality council homes, there has been a growing polarisation in the housing market. On the one hand, there is the ageing, poorer quality local authority sector for low-income groups and, on the other, the owner-occupied sector.

As council stock has declined and owner-occupation has remained or become out of the reach of many people, the number of homeless people has grown. The 1977 Homeless Persons Act requires local councils to house those without a home. In 1978 just under 60,000 households were accepted as homeless; ten years later the number of such households has doubled, involving 370,000 people (Shelter, 1988). Many of these are 'temporarily' housed in old barracks, disused schools or bed and breakfast hotels, with associated health risks.

These figures do not include those deemed to have made themselves homeless intentionally, or single homeless people. Despite recent concessions, there is still anxiety about the effects of benefit changes for 16–17-year-olds, which may lead to a rise in the numbers of homeless who are not officially recorded.

While the quality of housing does not exactly reflect the conventional class structure or socio-economic order, it is usually those who are already deprived who become homeless or who live in the poorest housing: single parents, the disabled, members of ethnic minorities, and the elderly.

30 JUNE 1989

Discussion Topic

Should homeless single people be covered by the Homeless Persons Act?

FURTHER READING

Murie, A. (1983) *Housing Inequality and Deprivation* (Heinemann).

Parker, J. and Mirrlees, C. (1988) 'Housing' in A.H. Halsey (ed.) *British Social Trends since 1900* (Macmillan).

Shelter (1988) *Raise the Roof*.

47

Winds of Change

What is Revolution?

On July 14 two hundred years ago the Paris mob stormed the Bastille. That same evening the Duc de la Rochefoucauld-Liancourt made an important conceptual distinction. 'Mais c'est une revolte', said Louis XVI. 'Non, sire, ce n'est pas une revolte', replied the Duc, 'c'est une revolution'.

Williams (1976) points out that the original meaning of the word 'revolution' concerns a revolving movement in space or time, as in the revolutions of the heavenly bodies. Its transition into the political context is gradual and complicated. Before the 17th century political acts against the established order were usually described as treason or, more commonly, rebellion or revolt, as in 'The Peasants' Revolt' or 'Wat Tyler's Rebellion'. Even Cromwell's military action against the monarchy was called, by its enemies, the 'Great Rebellion' whereas the less dramatic events of 1688 were called, by their supporters, the 'Glorious Revolution'.

Williams and others argue that the term revolution came to be used for the more substantial events because of the imagery of a wheel turning, with those on top cast down and those who were at the bottom taking over at the top.

This sense of an overturning of the established political order emerged during the 18th century. Until then, most political protests had involved demands for the restoration of rights or for the removal of an injustice or for the replacing of one elite group in power by another. The French Revolution changed all that.

This is not to say that the term revolution was never used in its modern sense before 1789. The American Revolution and Declaration of Independence in 1776 had involved a challenge to basic political values rather than just to a particular ruler. 'We hold these things to be self-evident . . . that all men are created equal . . .' was a profoundly revolutionary statement, akin to the French 'liberty, equality, fraternity'. But, says Williams, 'the specific effect of the French Revolution made decisive the modern sense of revolution', that of bringing about a 'wholly new social order'.

In the French and American cases, this new order was based on the belief that the revolution would restore the 'natural order' in which people who were born free would no longer be oppressed by kings or other autocratic leaders. As Thomas Paine put it in 1791: 'What we formerly called revolutions were little more than a change of persons . . . what we now see in the world from the revolutions of America and France are a renovation of the natural order of things'.

This belief in social progress and improvement through the revival of basic values also underlay the Iranian Revolution of 1978–9, whose declared intention was to restore the principles of Islam to their proper place in the modern world.

Giddens (1989) defines a revolution as 'the seizure of state power through violent means by the leaders of a mass movement, where that power is subsequently used to initiate major processes of social reform'. He distinguishes it from a *coup d'état*, which is the use of arms by individuals to seize power and replace existing leaders, but without radically changing the political system. A rebellion too, Giddens argues, aims to replace personnel rather than to transform the system.

A revolution necessarily involves the threat or the use of violence, rather than reform being achieved through persuasion and/or the ballot box. This definition implies that the concept of a non-violent revolution is a contradiction in terms, thus disqualifying, for example, the campaign of Mahatma Gandhi in India in the 1940s. Recent events in China fail to fit the definition on two counts; the leaders were essentially non-violent and they failed to seize power.

The 20th century has seen very many instances of revolutionary-type change, mostly in countries with predominantly peasant populations, of which probably the best known to English students are the Russian Revolution (1917) and the Chinese (1949). The frequency of modern revolutions has both been prompted by and given rise to various theories of revolution. Of course, the most important and influential is Marxism. However, American functionalism is also capable of explaining change, particularly revolutionary change.

Johnson (1983), for example, uses the theoretical model of Talcott Parsons to construct a theory of revolution. Parsons regards societies as systems which regulate themselves to maintain equilibrium. Johnson looks for the key to understanding revolutions in the breakdown of these self-regulating systems. This occurs when the system of economic production gets out of line with the central values and cultural system of a society. This leads to a state of disequilibrium, when the mass of the people become discontented.

The authorities can then attempt to retain control by restoring equilibrium through reforms or through the use of oppression. Both can avert revolution but the latter cannot do so indefinitely. Sooner or later the armed forces will become disloyal and either civil war or revolution becomes inevitable. The new political leaders then restore equilibrium.

Comparing the many 20th-century revolutions, almost all contemporary theorists argue that they have occurred not when conditions are at their worst but when they appear to be getting better but not quickly enough, or to have suffered a sudden deterioration. This idea is summarised in the concept of relative deprivation: it is not deprivation as such that causes discontent, but a sense of deprivation in comparison with what people have come to expect.

Such deprivation is not necessarily material; it may focus on the desire for equality or democracy (as in contemporary China). Even then, however, we have to explain how such discontent becomes mobilised into a mass movement, which may become violent and so revolutionary.

14 JULY 1989

Discussion Topic

How useful is Johnson's theory in explaining recent events in China?

FURTHER READING

Giddens, A. (1989) *Sociology* (Polity Press).

Johnson, C. (1983) *Revolutionary Change* (Longman).

Williams, R. (1976) *Keywords* (Fontana)

48

A Healthy State

The link between standards of health and social class has been known, in broad terms, since at least the middle of the last century. Since the late 1970s, however, the amount of research in this area has increased enormously, as has the sophistication of the techniques used for measuring ill-health.

The study of clinically defined disease in human populations is called epidemiology and has three main areas of concern. First, there are questions about the varying extent to which disease affects different groups of people (for example, social classes, ethnic groups, age groups, the sexes, married and single people).

Second, epidemiology looks at the causes of disease, which may be revealed by studying the patterns of its distribution. An early example of this was John Snow's study of the cholera epidemic in London in 1854 which showed that the disease was particularly prevalent in the area around the Broad Street pump. From this he suggested, correctly, that the disease was spread by contaminated water.

Third, there is the study of how particular diseases spread and of the effect of different therapies. In recent years, epidemiology helped to establish the link between smoking and lung cancer, and it is a vital weapon in the fight against Aids.

In measuring ill-health, epidemiologists are faced with the familiar research problem of how to put their concepts into practice, that is, to identify indicators of people's state of health which make it possible to collect reliable data that can be statistically manipulated. There is much debate about what constitutes health, ill-health, illness and disease, but epidemiologists measure health in two main ways: through mortality and through morbidity.

Mortality rates are more commonly known as death rates. The crude annual death rate refers simply to the number of people who die during a year per thousand of population alive at the start of the year. In the UK in 1987, the crude death rate was 11.5 for men and 11.2 for women. A more useful measure is the age-specific death rate, which calculates the number of people who die per thousand in a particular age group. Thus the infant mortality rate tells us the number of deaths every year of infants under one year old per thousand registered live births. This measure, combined with social class, reveals the often-cited fact that children born in social class 5 suffer twice the infant mortality rate of those born in class 1. The same kind of data are used to calculate the average life-expectancy of different groups in the population at various ages.

Mortality statistics, giving age and cause of death, have been available for more than a hundred years. However, while death itself is certainly a reliable indicator of someone's state of health, mortality statistics have several shortcomings. First, they measure only fatal illnesses and omit less serious and/or chronic conditions. Second, the cause of death that is entered on a death certificate is the subjective judgement of the doctor. This is by no means always a straightforward decision and might differ depending on which doctor was making it or when it was made.

As life expectancy has increased in our society, so mortality statistics have become less informative about the health of people under 70 years. Instead, measures of morbidity, the amount and distribution of ill-health, have become more widely used. But these are fraught with problems.

One source of such statistics are the records kept by general practitioners and by hospitals. In the case of GPs, the key point to recognise is that what a doctor records is the outcome of a sequence of interpretative events rather than a simple objective process of recording. First, individuals have to perceive themselves as being in a state where a visit to the doctor is appropriate. Sometimes this decision will be virtually automatic but, more often, it will be affected by their subjective interpretation (influenced by those around them) of their own state of health and of what is normal for someone of their age and social circumstances; by their judgement about whether the doctor can do anything for them and about whether the consequences of a diagnosis of disease are in fact desirable; and by the ease or difficulty with which they can arrange to see the doctor.

Once they are in the consulting room, the question of whether they are ill becomes a matter for negotiation with the doctor. There is much evidence that diagnosis is not an exact science, and doctors vary both among themselves and over time in the diagnostic decisions they make. The General Practice Morbidity Survey has the same potential shortcomings.

Hospital records, including the Hospital In-Patient Enquiry which collects data on 10 per cent of patients, are similarly affected by a host of social and economic circumstances. For example, the use of hospital facilities is partly a consequence of availability. If people know their local hospital has acquired a scanner, they and their GPs are more likely to arrange a scan and disease is more likely to be found.

Another source of morbidity statistics are self-report surveys, such as the General Household Survey, which collect data about people's subjective assessment of their health. In interpreting this data, it must be recognised that people's tolerance of symptoms varies.

An important area of current research is the relationship between self-reported illness and clinically assessed disease. People can feel ill without having any clinical symptoms, or can have a clinical pathology without feeling ill. There is also research into more objective indicators of health such as birth-weight, height and obesity. And there is work which defines ill-health in terms of the restriction, if any, on a person's normal activity, that is, on disability. The holy grail of such research would be an indicator which successfully combined a number of reliable indicators in a way which truly reflects people's real experience.

6 OCTOBER 1989

Discussion Topic

Who decides whether you are 'really' ill? Does it vary?

FURTHER READING

Aggleton, P. (1990) *Health* (Routledge).

Macintyre, S. (1986) 'Health and Illness' in R. Burgess, *Key Variables in Social Investigation* (RKP).

49

Poor Lore

The Emergence of the Underclass

Frank Field's new book *Losing Out: the Emergence of Britain's Underclass* (Blackwell) documents how far the poorest members of our society have fallen behind the rest of the community. The poor may, as the old cliché has it, be always with us, but to call them an underclass is to imply not only that they are at the bottom of the class structure, but also that they are both detached and excluded from mainstream society.

The concept of an underclass has its origins in the writings of Marx, who referred to a 'surplus population' in capitalist society. He included in this group older workers who lose their jobs, farmworkers who are seeking to move into industrial work, people in casual and irregular employment, people who cannot work, and the 'lumpenproletariat' – criminals, prostitutes and vagrants. Marx identified some of these groups as constituting a reserve army of labour, which is taken into employment when there is an economic boom and quickly discarded when there is a slump.

More recently, the concept of an underclass has been used to analyse the situation of ethnic minorities. Gunnar Myrdal in *An American Dilemma* (1944) described how black people in the US are not only pushed into a situation of failure but also lose their motivation to succeed. He stressed that this despair is a result of their experience, not of their personal or racial characteristics. This kind of analysis was echoed by writers in the 1950s and 1960s who described a 'culture of poverty' among the poor, whereby they failed to participate in the wider society and seemed fatalistic and reluctant to change.

Critics of this view argued that it amounted to blaming the victim and distracted attention from the economic structures which create poverty in the first place. Where the poor are also members of ethnic minorities, the 'culture of poverty' thesis was condemned as racist.

Anthony Giddens, in his study of *The Class Structure of the Advanced Societies* (1973), argued that an underclass exists when a group's economic position (its class) is superimposed on its status position, for example its ethnic origins. His major example was the US where blacks and Hispanics constitute the bulk of the underclass. Giddens did not expect that this group would ever be a force for revolutionary change but wrote: 'We may undoubtedly expect chronic "hostile outbursts" on the part of members of the underclass in so far as they are denied access to the exercise of "citizenship rights", on a par with white workers, in the economic and political spheres'. Such outbursts had already occurred in the US in the 1960s but were ten years away in the UK.

Rex and Tomlinson (1979) pick up the theme of how class position and status position overlap to create an underclass consisting of West Indian and Asian ethnic minorities in Britain. They show how their inferior position in the class structure, linked to their immigrant status and low economic position, is compounded by racism. They reject the 'culture of poverty' thesis, arguing that members of the underclass organise and protect themselves through their own communities rather than through the traditional political channels of the working class.

Dahrendorf (*New Statesman*, 12 June 1987) stressed the erosion of citizenship as the key characteristic of a newly-emergent underclass in Britain, which suffers from

'A cumulation of social pathologies. Members of the underclass tend to have a low level of educational attainment; many have not finished school; there is much functional and even absolute illiteracy. Incomplete families are the rule rather than the exception. Housing conditions for the underclass are usually miserable; to some extent, this class is an inner-city phenomenon . . . It is also a phenomenon of race.'

He places about 5 per of the population of Britain in the underclass, with twice that proportion in the US.

Field uses the term 'underclass' more loosely than his predecessors, and emphasises how the underclass has become separated from the rest in the past ten years. His underclass is made up of the long-term unemployed, single-parent families and elderly pensioners. He does not stress an ethnic dimension.

All these writers agree, with varying degrees of relief or disappointment, that there is no revolutionary potential in the underclass. They also agree, however, that members of this class are disproportionately involved in criminal activity, in riots and in other forms of mass violence. They feel that these people have little sense of duty towards the society which excludes them and in which they have no stake.

However, while there is general agreement as to the existence of the problem, there is a range of views across the political spectrum as to a solution.

Dahrendorf believes that 'the existence of an underclass violates the fundamental assumption of modern free societies that everyone without exception is a citizen with certain entitlements common to all'. He also takes the pragmatic line that the criminal and anti-social behaviour of the underclass is a threat to the stability of British society. His solution lies in locally-based community development programmes.

Field stresses the moral injustice of the continued existence of this group and argues for a programme of 'ethical socialism' including a return to full employment, taxation in order to reverse Thatcherite policies which have favoured the better-off, and reforms of the welfare state.

Saunders (1990) focuses on the underclass's dependence on state welfare benefits which, he says, destroys self-respect and feeds the culture of fatalism. 'The challenge for social policy in the 1990s', he writes, 'is to find ways of enabling the self-help of the underclass rather than offering yet more help from outside'. They should be empowered, through tax and voucher schemes, to determine their own priorities and to make choices.

20 OCTOBER 1989

Discussion Topic

How valid is it to regard women as constituting an underclass?

FURTHER READING

Rex, J. and Tomlinson, S. (1979) *Colonial Immigrants in a British City* (RKP).

Saunders, P. (1990) *Social Class and Stratification* (Routledge).

50

Party Lines

Parties and Pressure Groups

The textbooks will tell you that the annual conferences of the political parties are about party activists debating and formulating policy to be put into effect by the party executive. In recent years, the conferences of the major parties, especially the Conservatives, have been more carefully stage-managed than in the past, with their prime consideration the impression made on the TV viewer as potential voter.

The parties strive to portray themselves as democratic organisations which welcome lively debate, while at the same time ensuring that such debate does not become too lively. That would make it possible for rivals to suggest that the party is internally divided or that the leadership is at odds with the rank and file. The 1989 conferences demonstrated the major parties' growing skills in fostering an image of unity.

It is still the case that the aim of political parties in a democracy is to aggregate a range of policies on a variety of issues so as to command the support of enough voters to win a majority at elections. This is the key difference between parties and pressure groups. Pressure groups are also in the business of formulating policies but they concentrate on a single issue or on the interests of a single group of people.

Rather than seeking to gain power and form a government, pressure groups aim to influence those in government as well as the civil service, local government and public opinion. Thus, for example, a 'sectional' (or 'protective') pressure group such as the Confederation of British Industry protects the interests and publicises the views of business people on any issue that concerns them. A 'promotional' (or 'attitude') group promotes a cause, as in the case of the British Field Sports Society which defends field sports and opposes hostile legislation.

Members of sectional groups usually belong to the group whose interests, typically economic, are being protected, and usually come from similar socio-economic backgrounds. Promotional groups have members from a wider variety of backgrounds drawn together by their strong feelings on a particular issue, such as the people of Kent who are opposing the current proposals for the Channel Tunnel rail link.

There is sometimes overlap between promotional and sectional groups, as with groups whose support for a good cause also serves the interests of a particular group of people. In some of these groups, such as the Royal National Institute for the Blind and the Spastics Society, there can be tension over the fact that such groups are largely run for people with disabilities by the able-bodied. Arguably they should be run both *by* and *for* the people whose interests are being promoted. In other cases, such as the British Hedgehog Protection Society, this problem does not arise.

There are also instances where the distinction between party and pressure group is not clear-cut. For example, the Green Party's role until early 1989 had been more like that of the pressure groups from which it had sprung. The Greens aimed to inform and to change public opinion and official policy rather than having any realistic short-term expectation of gaining direct political power. The local and the European elections changed all that and the role of the Green Party changed with it. As its electoral success has increased, so it has had to formulate and present policies on the full range of contemporary political issues, rather than just the environment.

Opponents have derided it as a 'single-issue' party, which is an indirect way of calling it a pressure group. The Greens' response has been to acknowledge that many of their policies are as yet under-developed but to insist that there is a coherent Green line. This does not favour sectional interests, as do the major parties, and can be worked through on every issue from national security to the welfare state.

Now that the Greens are a legitimate political party with a solid rating in the opinion polls, they have begun to acquire the trappings and the problems of one, as was apparent at the 1989 conference. Their insistence that they have no individual leader, their way of conducting conference business, and the apparent naivety (or was it honesty?) of some of their spokespersons laid them open to ridicule from those who wanted to rubbish their policies. Similarly, there were accusations from their own ranks that electoral success was already causing the leadership to compromise the ideological purity of the party.

Nevertheless, as long as the Greens have no immediate prospect of forming a government, their role will continue to be more like that of a pressure group, but one which the major parties cannot afford to ignore.

The Labour Party conference demonstrated the problem of being an organisation that has been described as 'two thirds pressure group, one third political party'. The origins of the Labour Party lie in the organisation of working people in trade unions in the 19th century. The unions, which are sectional pressure groups, are still vital to the success of the party. The problem for the Labour leadership is that if they wish to gain power they have to come up with policies that will appeal to a much larger proportion of the population.

What makes this task more difficult is the increasingly loose link between people's occupational class and their voting habits. This leads to many of the rows and splits which are so gleefully played up by the Tory press. Changes in Labour policy in recent years, as the influence of union leaders such as Arthur Scargill has waned, represent an attempt to mobilise the votes of people who have little connection with the traditional working class. The unity which marked the 1989 conference can be seen as a success for the party managers in minimising public conflict between the electoral ambitions of the party leaders and the sectional interests of the pressure group.

27 OCTOBER 1989

Discussion Topic

Are the nationalist parties also pressure groups?

FURTHER READING

Coxall, W.N. (1986) *Parties and Pressure Groups* (Longman).

51

Growing Up

Children's Rights

Which group of people in our society is not allowed to choose where to live, to dispose of its own property, to consume alcohol or to smoke, to take a full-time job, to drive, or to engage in sexual activity? Which group can be physically assaulted, even in public, without the law necessarily being involved, and can legally be confined to a building for seven hours a day?

The answer is 'children'. Most of the prohibitions are made in the name of protecting children from their own inexperience, but some aspects of some children's experience suggest that what they need protection from is adults. In these terms, the new UN Convention on the Rights of the Child is overdue. It is concerned with children world-wide, and perhaps we tend to think of it as applying to Third World countries, but it is just as relevant to the United Kingdom.

It is an axiom of sociology that social roles and behaviour are more the outcome of social context than they are of biology. Gender roles, for example, are seen as being socially constructed, as in the inferior status of ethnic minorities in society. The same applies to the various age-categories into which people are placed.

If the way adults behave towards children and the way they respond were biologically determined, then it would be much the same in all societies. Historical and comparative studies show that this is not the case. No one is claiming that physical characteristics have no effect at all on how people are treated. It is the social interpretation of, and the response to, these characteristics that has changed historically and still varies both between and within societies.

The debate about the social construction of childhood in industrial societies was launched by the social historian Philippe Aries. According to Aries (1960) the modern notion of childhood has its origins in about the 15th century. Before then, there was of course a socially recognised period of infancy, but in medieval times young people from about the age of five years were treated as miniature adults. Their social obligations were much the same as those of adults, though limited by their physical size, and they were integrated into the adult world of work and of leisure.

From the 17th century, and with considerable variation between the offspring of the rich and of the poor, and boys and girls, young people began to be treated differently from their elders. Starting with the sons of the wealthy, children began to be segregated into a separate social world, a process which began to gather pace in the 19th century.

This was marked by restrictions being placed on the employment of children and by the spread of education, though these changes did not substantially affect working-class children until the last quarter of the century. At the same time, children's rights in matters of the ownership of property were limited. The first laws forbidding cruelty to children were passed exactly one hundred years ago, and from 1908 children were placed under a separate system of criminal justice. The courts were empowered to place neglected or maltreated children into the care of the local authority. By the 20th century, the social category of the child was distinctly defined.

Aries's work has not gone unchallenged. For example, it has been pointed out that, as a historian, his sources are mostly limited to those of the wealthy and literate strata of society, and that we know little about the lives of the children of the mass of the population. The historical evidence is also from the male standpoint and medieval mothers may have been more aware of child/adult differences than fathers were.

But what of children in our society today? What would an Aries of the future or a contemporary visiting anthropologist note about the status and role of children in Britain?

They would surely be struck by how far children are dependent on adults for virtually all their needs, both material and emotional. In relationships of dependency, the independent person has power over the dependent (Article 18). Where there is such an imbalance of power, there is the risk of the abuse of power. Our visiting anthropologist would find it relatively easy to account for the existence of child abuse.

She would observe, too, that the period of compulsory education, which ensures economic dependency, is being effectively lengthened into the early twenties for those aiming at a professional career and, for the less academic, via the mechanisms of the Youth Training Scheme, with its associated rules about state benefits.

Our imaginary researcher would also notice the massive commercial activity which centres on children as consumers and on adults, especially women, as consumers on behalf of children. In researching this, the extent of poverty among children would become apparent.

A competent social observer would also become aware that the experience of childhood varies by social class, by gender, by ethnicity and by area of residence. The seven-year-old daughter of a farm worker in rural Wales leads a very different life from that of Prince Harry.

The researcher would also become aware of the vast amount of legislation that concerns children, much of it passed since the Second World War, and particularly in the 1970s. The manifest intention of this legislation has been to meet the needs and to protect the interests of children.

A latent effect has been to expand the role of the state. As in other fields, care and control go hand in hand.

But what above all characterises childhood in our society is the inconsistency between the values and attitudes that most people express about children and the way in which many children are actually treated.

The new UN Convention is as relevant to us as it is to other societies.

24 NOVEMBER 1989

Discussion Topic

Compare the status of mentally handicapped people to that of children in our society.

FURTHER READING

Aries, P. (1960) *Centuries of Childhood* (Penguin).
O'Donnell, M. (1985) *Age and Generation* (Tavistock).

52

Home Truths

The Experience of Homelessness

The word 'home' like 'family' 'motherhood' and 'community', refers to
an aspect of social life where myth and reality may sharply diverge. The
connotations of the myth are so positive that to point out the negative
aspects of the reality seems almost perverse. 'Home sweet home', 'home
is where the heart is', 'the old folks at home'; they are all the same. We
even have a Home Office rather than a Ministry for Internal Affairs.

If you ask someone the question 'what makes your home your
home?' they will answer not in terms of bricks and mortar but in terms
of feelings of security, of privacy, of possessions, and of home being the
place where you can choose your companions or be alone, do what you
like and be yourself. A home is not a house but a set of relationships and
a sense of belonging. It involves both rights and obligations. Robert
Frost saw this when he wrote:
'Home is the place where, when you have to go there,
They have to let you in'.
'I should have called it
Something you somehow haven't to deserve'.

(*Death of a Hired Man*)

If 'home' is the positive value, then 'homelessness' is the negative.
But the reality of home life for many people is very different from the
myth. If you are ever physically assaulted, even murdered, it is most
likely to take place in your home. The strongest emotions, including
anger, hate, and fear are experienced within the home. Young people
who have 'run away from home' have often pulled out of a situation
that was the opposite of what home life is supposed to be.

Their subjective experience of being without a home started long
before they physically left. The core of their homelessness, at least at
first, is not economic but emotional. Returning to the parental home in
the physical sense will not relieve this.

The ambivalent nature of the idea of home is further demonstrated
by changing the initial letter from a small h to a capital H. Homes for
the elderly are so called in an attempt to project a positive image, and
perhaps in the hope that the reality will result from the naming. However,

whereas many staff working in Homes are taken in by this and resist the suggestion that they are working in institutions, the prospective and actual residents are not deceived. 'I don't want to go into a Home: I want to stay in my home'. 'This is your home, dear', says the care assistant, but it isn't.

The sense of home as a place of belonging and as a secure base seems to be common to all cultures. In modern societies, the notion of home also implies staying in one place. Nomadism is regarded as 'primitive'. To settle down, we assume, is a prerequisite for civilisation.

But to be nomadic is not necessarily to be homeless. The temporary shelters of the hunting Bushmen of the Kalahari were of the lightest possible construction, but they were not the centre of their world. '"Home", for the greater part of the year, was wherever he made a major kill. Nonetheless, he had a permanent base on which his whole life swung' (van der Post, 1962). These were round walls some four or five feet high, inside which the Bushmen would make a fire, cook and sleep. Where they could, the Bushmen made their home under an overhanging rock or in a cave. This is where their art, music and painting thrived.

The nomads of our society are the traveller-gypsies. 'In terms of a house-dwelling ideology, caravans are defined as makeshift transient eyesores; either temporary holiday accommodation or proof of inadequate municipal housing provision' (Okely, 1983). To use a caravan as a truly mobile home is symbolically to subvert the dominant view which dictates that civilised people live in one place. Public and official reaction to gypsies reveals how great a challenge they are to people's sense of what is proper. But the gypsies, moving in families and groups, take their sense of home around with them. Their security of belonging in a set of stable relationships is stronger than that of many house-dwellers.

But is the norm of living in our society in fact so static? Peter Berger *et al.* (1973) use the metaphor of homelessness to describe the alienated condition of people in modern societies. In such societies more and more people's lives are migratory and ever-changing. People switch rapidly between a variety of social contexts, which are often contradictory to each other.

This makes certainty on matters of ethics and truth more difficult to achieve. Religion no longer provides the positive guidance that it used to. 'Because of the religious crisis in modern society, social homelessness has become metaphysical – that is, it has become homelessness in the cosmos. This is very difficult to bear'.

Lacking a sense of belonging, people try to find or to create a home by divorcing their public from their private life, and then seek meaning in the latter in an attempt to compensate for the discontents of the former. But private life, says Berger, cannot provide the wider structures and the supports that people need.

Modernisation has certainly freed people from the narrow confines of family, clan and tribe. It has opened up endless choices and possibilities. But we do pay a price for this freedom: the loss of a sense of belonging. That is why, the Bergers say, people who are trying to escape from meaninglessness and alienation are often attracted to demodernising movements, such as the New Age religions.

As John Berger (*New Society*, 23 June 1983) puts it: 'At its most brutal, home is no more than your name – while to most people you are nameless.' Whether in cosmological terms, in the more mundane terms of being homeless on the streets of London, or for the inmates of institutions, having no one know your name is perhaps the essence of homelessness.

1 DECEMBER 1989

Discussion Topic

'Home is the girl's prison and the woman's workhouse' (G.B. Shaw). Discuss.

FURTHER READING

Berger, P., Berger, B. and Kellner, H. (1973) *The Homeless Mind* (Random House).

Okely, J. (1983) *The Traveller-Gypsies* (Cambridge).

van der Post, L. (1962) *The Lost World of the Kalahari* (Penguin).

53

School Secrets

The Hidden Curriculum

The students of the late 1980s are the last generation to experience 16 to 19 education as it is organised at present. In December 1989, the Secretary of State for Education, John MacGregor (with the backing of Norman Fowler, the Employment Secretary) called upon the National Curriculum Council to come up by March 1990 with a specification for a core curriculum of compulsory studies for all 16 to 19-year-olds. The idea is to bridge the gulf that exists between academic and vocational courses.

The core will include communications, information technology, numeracy and modern foreign languages. It must be studied by all students in the age group, whether they are taking vocational courses such as B/TEC or an academic course which includes A and A/S levels. In due course, whatever is agreed will be incorporated into the new framework being developed by the National Council for Vocational Qualifications.

These proposals are the latest step in the most far-reaching review of the curriculum in schools and colleges that the UK has ever seen. Naturally enough, the reforms have attracted a great deal of attention from sociologists of education, especially those concerned with the sociology of knowledge. There has been less attention paid to what in the 1960s and 1970s was known as the 'hidden curriculum'.

The phrase was first used by Jackson in *Life in Classrooms* (1964) and refers to all those things pupils learn in schools that are not overtly taught. These are mainly attitudes, values and principles of behaviour which, though not explicitly spelled out by teachers, are rewarded when pupils display them through their actions.

The hidden curriculum can be found in the way that a school is organised, in the way that teachers and pupils interact, and in the content of the subjects taught.

Most schools are organised in a hierarchy of authority. There is not much doubt about who is in charge or about how decisions are made. The more taken-for-granted such hierarchies are, the less likely it is that pupils will question whether this is an appropriate way to run an organisation, or indeed to organise society as a whole. And yet 'progressive' schools like Summerhill or Dartington Hall have always tried to ensure that pupils participate in decision-making. They claim that pupils learn to take responsibility for their own actions, for each other, and for their community.

Even the physical layout of the traditional classroom, with the teacher dominant at the front of the room, controlling the blackboard and able to see all that happens, encourages pupils to internalise a view of themselves as inferior and subject to those more powerful. Open-plan classrooms or workshop systems suggest a different pupil-teacher relationship, though the teacher is still in charge.

School uniforms can be interpreted in the same way. Those who support the wearing of uniform, usually adults, stress that it encourages pupils to develop loyalty to the group. They argue that a uniform conceals the inequalities of income among pupils which would be revealed if they could all choose what to wear to school. Opponents of uniform emphasise that it symbolises the arbitrary power that schools exercise over pupils. Once pupils are in uniform they become subject to that power, just as if they were in the army or a penal institution. This view is reinforced by observing the importance pupils attach to subversion of the uniform by wearing tatty ties, shortening hemlines or undoing a top button. Similarly, why do some teachers get so angry about such apparently minor rule-breaking? They know, at some level, that it is a challenge to the whole power-structure of the school.

The hidden curriculum is also traceable within the mainstream curriculum, which reflects an élitist, male and ethnocentric view of what is worthwhile knowledge. Those who favour multi-cultural education point out that a course in literature that studies only English writers is indirectly saying that African and Asian writers are not worthy of scholarly attention. If the course were called English Literature it would at least be more accurate. But why should literary studies be limited in this way?

Similarly, a history that places the UK at the centre of world events is implying that this is the normal or even the only valid viewpoint. Feminist scholars have shown how women are systematically devalued in the curriculum, usually by simple omission of any account of their role in history, the arts, or science.

The concept of the hidden curriculum was particularly attractive in the 1970s to those sociologists, often though not always Marxist, who argued that the official rhetoric of schools is at odds with their real function in a capitalist society. At that time, the dominant view of education stressed that it should be pupil-centred and foster the development of individual potential, with little emphasis on preparation for work. Those who underlined the role of the hidden curriculum were saying that this liberal message was a sham. Mass schooling was in fact in the business of doing what it had always done – reinforcing the values and attitudes which allowed the individual to be easily absorbed into an alienated and unequal society.

Critics have suggested that the hidden curriculum was hidden from academic sociologists more than from its victims, who knew very well what was happening. It is also more useful to think of it as intertwined with rather than concealed behind the mainstream curriculum. But recent and future reforms of how education is organised suggest that some aspects of the hidden curriculum are not so hidden any more.

We now see the official fragmentation of knowledge into the ten subjects of the core curriculum; the massive extension of assessment; the devaluing of non-vocational subjects; the belief in market forces as the key to anything worthwhile. All these demonstrate the substantial change in educational priorities over the last 15 years. They certainly lay to rest the old claim that education is not a political activity.

5 JANUARY 1990

Discussion Topic

What is the hidden curriculum of your sociology syllabus?

54

Hate Attack

Black People's Experience of Crime

'Despite the progress made, racism and its most ugly manifestations, racial attacks and harassment, are still frightening realities for many British citizens.' With these words in its report, published on 20 December 1989, the Home Affairs Select Committee of the House of Commons confirmed yet again the reality of racism in Britain today. And racial attacks are not the whole story, for Asians and Afro-Caribbeans are at significantly greater risk of becoming victims of all types of crime than are white people.

Until recently, only partial sketches of the extent of racial harassment have been available. Such data as did exist could not be combined to make up a more complete picture because the research had been done in different ways. Thus, in 1981 a Home Office study found that Asians were 50 times and Afro-Caribbeans 36 times more likely to be racially victimised. This study only recorded cases reported to the police, and there is plenty of evidence that people are unwilling to report such incidents. Five years later, a survey in the London Borough of Newham concluded that police statistics recorded only one in 20 racial attacks occurring there. It found 116 ethnic minority victims reporting 1550 incidents, nearly as many as were officially recorded in the Metropolitan Police district for the whole year.

However, the Home Office's 1988 British Crime Survey provided for the first time an authoritative national picture of the greater likelihood of Asian and Afro-Caribbean people becoming victims of crime. The BCS is a victim survey, and measures the crimes people say they have experienced in the course of a year (see Article 65). The 1988 survey especially boosted the numbers of Asians and Afro-Caribbeans interviewed to obtain a representative sample of those communities.

Its findings, which divided crimes into 'personal' and 'household', were startling. Afro-Caribbeans and Asians were more likely to be victims of all types of crime (including assaults, threats and robbery) than white people. Asians were more likely to experience virtually all types of household crime, including burglary, vandalism and theft from vehicles. Afro-Caribbeans, too, were more likely than whites to be victims of most types of household crime.

Racial motivation was clearly an important factor. The survey followed the practice of all police forces, in recording as racially motivated any incident where the victim identified that as the cause. Asians said 24 per cent, and Afro-Caribbeans 15 per cent, of the crimes against them were racially motivated. The use of racist language by the perpetrator was the most frequent reason for inferring the motive.

The Home Office researchers explain some of this by pointing out that the ethnic minority population in Britain has proportionately more young people, who are always over-represented in crime statistics, and also that Asians and Afro-Caribbeans are more likely to live in a deprived neighbourhood with a higher crime state. Although this does modify the pattern, there remains a tendency for ethnic minorities to experience more serious crimes than white people.

What needs to be done in response to these figures? Over the last two years, the Metropolitan Police have reacted in a number of ways. Tackling racial attacks has been made a declared priority for the Met and for three other forces. This has been backed up by a force order instructing officers to treat incidents seriously, to use a charge of Actual Bodily Harm rather than the less severe Common Assault, and to use Section 5 of the 1986 Public Order Act, where 'harassment, alarm or distress' has been caused. In addition, cases of racial harassment are now supervised at a more senior level.

Although the police often have the primary role, racial harassment requires a response from many agencies working together, as shown by a recent Home Office interdepartmental working group. Education authorities, social services departments and, in particular, housing departments, all have a role to play. Several have added racial harassment as a ground for eviction under their tenancy agreements. On the rare occasions where this has been used, however, the results have been mixed. Departments are unsure whether to treat those evicted as intentionally homeless, and so ineligible for alternative council accommodation. From the voluntary sector, the National Association of Victim Support Schemes is running a two-year project to help meet the needs of victims of racial attacks.

Much remains to be done if the full message of the British Crime Survey is to be heeded. Despite the fact that Asian and Afro-Caribbean people are at greater risk from all types of crime, whether racially motivated or not, the police and other agencies still concentrate on harassment.

In 1988, the Commission for Racial Equality sponsored a report on policing and racial equality. *Fair Cop* advocated that the Metropolitan Police should boost equal opportunities throughout the service, rather than concentrate on dealing with racial harassment or ethnic minority recruitment. Although the Commissioner welcomed the report at the time, few of its recommendations have been followed.

The effectiveness of the Met's racial harassment force order has not been publicly evaluated. There is some evidence that the Crown Prosecution Service has not pursued police recommendations on the prosecution of racial attackers. A recent information campaign by the Met was an expensive flop, with many glossy brochures left undelivered.

Ethnic minority people await an effective response from the authorities to all types of crime. Police, local authorities and the Crown Prosecution Service still need to rethink their approach.

19 JANUARY 1990

Discussion Topic

How useful is it to treat vulnerability to crime as an aspect of social disadvantage?

FURTHER READING

1988 British Crime Survey (1989) (HMSO).

Glare: *Fair Cop* (1989) (CRE).

The Newham Crime Survey (1987) (London Borough of Newham).

55

Female Trouble

Women and Crime

What was so outrageous about Judge James Pickles imprisoning 19-year-old Tracey Scott at the end of 1989? Why was there such an outcry before the Appeal Court released her? She had pleaded guilty to helping shoplifters in the systematic theft of £4000 worth of goods from the store where she worked on the checkout. Along with two others, she simply failed to ring up the purchases on the tills through which the thieves passed.

The theft was premeditated, and £4000 is a lot of money. The courts usually give heavy sentences in cases of theft which involve an abuse of trust. Six months' imprisonment is not a particularly long sentence for such an offence.

Part of the outcry was because this was Ms Scott's first offence. But what really prompted the public reaction was that she had a ten-week-old baby and that Judge Pickles commented, when sentencing, that he wished to deter young women from becoming pregnant in the period between being charged and appearing in court in the hope that this would save them from a prison sentence.

Our male-dominated judicial system has for many years found itself in difficulties dealing with women charged or convicted of crime. A common response, shared by many academic criminologists, was to define such women as ill rather than criminal and so in need of treatment rather than punishment.

This 'illness' response often involved linking women's criminality with the female reproductive system, so that shoplifting was associated with the stereotype of the menopausal woman, and violence with premenstrual tension or post-natal depression. Certainly, female teenage delinquency was never explained in the familiar male terms of 'natural exuberance'. Even female terrorism, as in the cases of Ulrike Meinhof or of Patty Hearst, tended to be explained in terms of the women falling in love with or being sexually dominated by a man. This seemed preferable to an alternative explanation: that a woman might resort to terrorism for the same calculated reasons as a man.

The fact that so few women feature in the official statistics of crime helped make it possible to treat them as a small and sick minority. In England and Wales in 1987, for example, whereas 339,200 men were sentenced for indictable offences (broadly the more serious ones), only 47,500 women were so sentenced. The women's offences were, overall, both less serious and less numerous. Even in the case of shoplifting, often cited as the classic female crime, convictions are shared roughly equally between the sexes, with men stealing larger and more expensive items. Also in 1987, where 160 per 100,000 men over 21 in England and Wales were sentenced to gaol, only six women per 100,000 were so sentenced. In contrast, victim surveys and self-report studies show that women feature far more extensively as victims of crime, especially violent crime.

However, until the appearance of feminist literature on crime from the late 1960s, the great majority of criminological research simply ignored female criminals. Variables such as social class, IQ, educational achievement, poverty and upbringing were all identified by research as the key causal factor for (male) crime. But no study took the near-absence of women seriously as a potential key to the explanation of (male) criminality. Sex, the most reliable single variable in the prediction of criminality, was largely ignored.

The issue was addressed by some writers, of whom perhaps the most notorious is Pollak. He argued, in 1961, that the relative absence of women from criminal statistics was explained not by their lack of criminal activity but by their success in evading detection. Women's inherent facility to deceive was demonstrated, he said, by their ability to fake orgasm and their need to conceal menstruation and pregnancy.

The paucity of women in the figures has also been explained by a 'chivalry factor'. Some researchers have argued that the police treat women offenders more leniently than men, giving more informal cautions, and that the courts are less willing to sentence a woman to any kind of detention. Research in the 1980s has generally not supported this claim.

The notion of a chivalry factor contrasts with evidence that the authorities' reaction to women offenders varies according to their alleged offence. Some offences, especially crimes of violence, place the woman in 'double jeopardy'. She is punished not only for the offence, as a man would be, but more severely because she is seen as having behaved 'unnaturally'.

This may be part of the reason why Myra Hindley has received so much more media attention than Ian Brady, her partner in the Moors murders. In fact, her media portrayal has varied over the 26 years since the murders. Contemporary accounts, including Emlyn Williams' *Beyond Belief*, suggested that she had been sexually dominated by Brady, who was the ringleader. The more attention Hindley has received, the more her image has become that of an evil woman, even as the dominant partner who used her sexuality to corrupt Brady.

Recent research suggests that the small numbers of women in the criminal statistics has the simplest explanation. Women commit fewer crimes, especially the more serious crimes. This then becomes the phenomenon to be explained, and feminist writers have sought an explanation in the male-dominated structure of our society and in the way in which women are socialised.

Judge Pickles seems to have been working with a model of Tracey Scott as a devious woman who abused her reproductive role to avoid her just deserts. The media response included a chivalry factor and invoked a model of woman-as-mother, an ideal which cannot easily be reconciled with that of thief and gaol bird.

26 JANUARY 1990

Discussion Topic

What models of womanhood are portrayed in your favourite soap opera?

FURTHER READING

Heidensohn, F. (1985) *Women and Crime* (Macmillan).

56

Off the Beat

> ## *The Changing Role of the Police*

The Taylor report on the Hillsborough disaster, which placed the blame firmly on the South Yorkshire police, was another heavy blow to their public image. At least, in that instance, the police were convicted only of incompetence, aggravated by a refusal to admit fault. That is perhaps an improvement on being shown as corrupt, in the case of the Guildford Four, or out of control, as at Wapping, or guilty of criminal assaults, as in recent cases where courts have awarded damages against the police. Whatever happened to the traditional British bobby, a figure known to student readers of this book only through old films?

Critchley, the best-known historian of the British police, traces their origins to the Saxon tythingman, who was the elected representative of a group of ten families and embodied the community's collective responsibility to apprehend and punish its own wrongdoers. This arrangement was much modified but its underlying ethos, says Critchley, lasted into the 18th century. It could not, however, survive the rapid social changes which resulted from the development of industrialism and the movement of populations into towns. This created the need for a specialist force.

Though the Bow Street Runners had been formed in London by the 1780s, the first proper police force in the UK, the Metropolitan Police, was established in 1829. By 1856 there were over 200 such forces in England and Wales. Their role was spelled out by Mayne in 1829 and reiterated by Lord Scarman in 1981: 'the prevention of crime . . . the protection of life and property, the preservation of public tranquillity'. The police are an arm of the state, which has a monopoly of the legitimate use of force in society and exercises it, according to this view, in the interests of the citizenry as a whole.

A more critical analysis of the creation of a specialist police force explains it as the result of the rise of capitalism rather than simply of industrialism. As a state agency, the police force necessarily operates in the interests of the ruling class. The maintenance of public order means the control of working-class resistance against its exploitation. The vigorous use of the police against the Luddites, the Chartists and later uprisings can be explained in this way. While the police help the working class as individuals to protect themselves against crime, they are opposed to the interests of the class as a whole. This helps to explain the ambivalent working-class attitude to the police described, for example, by Richard Hoggart in 1955: 'They tend to regard the policeman primarily as someone who is watching them, who represents the authority which has its eye on them, rather than as a member of the public services whose job it is to help protect them'.

In so far as the police are in the business of maintaining order and controlling deviance, theirs is undeniably a political role. However, the relative consensus and stability of the years after the Second World War made it possible to develop an image of the police as a non-political force. This image is now questioned on every side.

Reiner (1985) suggests that an improvement might have been expected. The police include a more representative cross-section of the population, including graduates and women; they are better-trained and equipped; they are, on balance, more accountable. And yet public attitudes have steadily worsened while mistrust and hostility have grown. Why is this?

Reiner identifies several interrelated causes. First, there were the bribery and corruption scandals of the 1970s. Mass dismissals and retirements have reduced these, but they have been replaced by cases of police abuse of power and faking of evidence. The disbanding of the West Midlands Regional Crime Squad in 1989 shows that the police recognise the scale of the problem, and great store is set by the Police and Criminal Evidence Act of 1984, which was intended to minimise the potential for corruption.

Next, the use of paramilitary style force by the police has grown, both in urban riots and in political demonstrations and industrial disputes such as the miners' strikes and at Wapping.

Senior policemen are now more ready to enter into public debate. The Conservative Party in particular has made law and order a party-political issue and senior policemen are thereby associated with Tory politics, especially as several Labour local authorities have taken strong anti-police stances on questions such as racial harassment.

Police personnel have come off the beat and become motorised. They use increasingly specialised and hi-tech equipment. They are more involved in plainclothes work; surveillance and intelligence. Increasingly, the police regard themselves as a profession and entitled, like other professions, to act beyond the control of lay people. Hence they insist that other officers should enquire into misconduct.

Above all, in terms of a deteriorating public image, the police are regarded as less and less effective at what the public sees as their main task – crime prevention and detection. Crime rates rise and clear-up rates fall.

Recent moves towards community policing are intended to restore the balance between a remote professional force keeping the populace under control and a public service for people in need of help. But the wider context of policing has also changed significantly. In the last 25 years, British society has again become deeply and overtly divided on social and economic lines, with increased industrial militancy, ethnic divisions, and the re-emergence of a deprived underclass. In addition, many members of the middle class have joined political and civil libertarian protest, which has brought them into conflict with the police for the first time.

Whether all this is seen as a crisis of capitalism or evidence of growing *anomie* in a rapidly changing world, a divided society is one in which the police have to take sides. Policing by universal consent is no longer possible, and policing by enforcement may be inevitable.

23 FEBRUARY 1990

Discussion Topic

What images of the police are promoted by 'The Bill'?

FURTHER READING

Reiner, R. (1985) *The Politics of the Police* (Wheatsheaf).

57

Crystal Balls

Population Projections

The twentieth edition of *Social Trends* was published in February 1990 and the occasion prompted its editor to make some forecasts about social and economic life in the UK for the next two decades.

By the year 2011, the population will be up to 60 million, compared to 57 million in 1988. Within this total, the number of 16-year-olds will fall from its present 800,000 to about 650,000 in 1991, will rise again to about 840,000 in 2011 and then decline to some 720,000 in the early 2020s.

How are such forecasts made and how accurate are they?

The main point to recognise is that they are *projections*; that is, forecasts of the future which are based on current evidence and on the trends of the recent past. They are extrapolations of a trend or of a supposed trend. To make a projection of the population in 2010, for example, the demographer notes the size of the present population and its age and sex structure, and then considers recent trends in birth-rates, death-rates and migration. All these are matters of historical record.

At this point, the demographer has to start making assumptions about whether these rates will rise, stay constant, fall or fluctuate over the next 20 years. A projection is literally a 'throwing forward', so the demographer throws current trends forward into the future. It is the assumptions that are made that determine the accuracy of the projection.

Tom Griffin, *Social Trends'* editor, is fully aware of this. He writes: 'It should of course be borne in mind that projections do not have the accuracy of historical statistics. They are all subject to revision as new evidence emerges and new assumptions are made'.

In fact, population forecasts in the postwar period have often turned out to be wrong. In the mid-sixties, the high birth-rate prompted predictions of a population of 73 million for Great Britain by the year 2000. Unless something completely extraordinary happens to birth-rates, death-rates and immigration, there is now no way that that total will be reached. By 1983, the projection was down to 56 million. Now it is up again. Current population forecasts for Britain tend to assume that fertility will remain at or just below replacement level until the end of the century, whereas in many other European countries it is expected to be below that level.

Projections of the number of 16-year-olds involve fewer assumptions. We know how many children there are of all ages up to fifteen, and the death-rates of this age group have been reasonably constant for some years. After allowing for a small amount of migration, it is possible then to forecast very accurately how many 16-year-olds there will be in each of the next 15 years. After that, demographers are dependent on knowing how many women of child-bearing age there will be in the population in each year, and then making projections about how many babies they will have.

Griffin uses the projection of the number of births outside marriage to suggest the dangers of naive extrapolation. If the recent increase in the number of such births were maintained at the current rate, for example, it would result in all births being outside marriage in less than 20 years. Though this idea was seized upon by the media, it is not going to happen because there are too many other variables involved.

Can such projections be self-fulling, or even self-defeating, prophecies?

It seems unlikely that knowledge of projected birth-rates will directly affect anyone's personal decision about whether to have a child. But it could affect government policies which may encourage or discourage birth-rates. In China in the 1970s, for example, a policy of 'one child per family' resulted in a lower birth-rate.

A more complex example is that of road traffic. *Social Trends* projects that, for every hundred miles driven by all motor traffic in 1988, somewhere between 170 and 222 miles will be covered in 2020. Cecil Parkinson, the Transport Secretary, argues that to deal with the increase more roads must be built. But new roads may simply encourage more traffic, as in the notorious example of the M25.

But, however provisional the projections may be, the fact that we can make them at all is powerful evidence of the orderliness and predictability of human social behaviour. Activities like having babies, getting married, or committing crimes are, at one level, personal and individual. But they occur in patterns which are broadly predictable. It is this orderliness on which the discipline of sociology is based.

This is the fundamental insight that Durkheim offered in *The Rules of Sociological Method* (1895) which enabled him to contribute to the establishment of modern sociology as a legitimate discipline. He called these regularities 'social facts' and defined them as 'ways of acting, thinking and feeling, external to the individual and endowed with a power of coercion by reason of which they control him'. He gives the examples of moral regulations, religious faiths, language, and financial systems.

He also describes as facts 'social currents', such as those that occur in crowd behaviour, and 'currents of opinion' which, he says, 'impel certain groups either to more marriages, for example, or to more suicides, or to a higher or lower birth-rate'. These can all be expressed statistically. Statistics absorb individual variation and, says Durkheim, 'the average expresses a certain state of the group mind'.

Durkheim's theorising of the concepts of a social fact and of a group mind was challenged right from the start (see his preface to the second edition of his book) and continues to be so. But, if these statistical regularities can be shown and future trends can be projected, then there is certainly something happening which cannot be explained simply as the sum of a mass of random individual actions.

9 MARCH 1990

Discussion Topic

What are the main factors affecting the birth-rate?

FURTHER READING

Durkheim, E. (1964) *The Rules of Sociological Method* (Free Press).
Social Trends 20 (1990) (HMSO).

58

Open Season

The Sociology of the Countryside

Two announcements were made early in 1990 which, between them, seem to epitomise an aspect of British social life today to which sociology has not yet paid enough attention.

First, the Transport Secretary, Cecil Parkinson, announced that part of the new M3 extension would be built in a cutting through Twyford Down, a beauty spot near Winchester. Local environmental groups have campaigned against such a plan for over 15 years, arguing in favour of tunnelling through in order to minimise the damage to the scenic beauty of the area and to the remains of Iron Age forts and other ancient sites. Such a conflict of interest is not unusual but it is significant that Mr Parkinson defended his proposed route by saying that it would be designed to run through agricultural land rather than through the open downland. Thirty years ago, the priorities might have been reversed.

The second announcement was that planning permission had been granted for the development of a massive 'theme park' on Rainham Marshes in Essex. The unsuccessful opposition to this proposal had come mainly from people interested in the marshes as an important habitat for birds and other wildlife.

Between them, these stories embrace all the major interests competing over the future of the countryside: farmers, developers, road-builders, ecologists, conservationists, the leisure industry, local residents, visitors, and people concerned with Britain's historical 'heritage'. Just as the contemporary countryside reflects past conflicts of interest, so the outcome of current conflicts will determine its future.

The discipline of sociology was born of the social turbulence of industrialisation. It has tended therefore to concentrate on urban issues. Rural sociology and the sociology of the countryside have been relatively neglected. From the 1930s there was a school of thought which tried to establish a link between settlement patterns and ways of life, arguing that there was a rural-urban continuum. But this model was discarded in the light of new research in 1960s. Since then, there have been very few specifically sociological attempts to explain the processes of rural change. The work of Howard Newby is the exception.

For centuries, the major role of the countryside was to provide food. Except for the wealthy nobility, able to indulge in hunting for recreation, the rural population regarded the land primarily as a workplace. Country people depended, directly or indirectly, on agriculture for their major source of income, in cash or in kind, and were relatively unconcerned with questions of natural beauty. The notion of landscape-as-beauty was a creation of the rich in the 18th century, when they constructed parks and views to match the ideal images of the landscape painters of the time. The functional activity of farming was not allowed to intrude into these picturesque vistas, unless suitably contrived to add to the merits of the view from the terrace of the great house.

Towards the end of the 19th century, the major threat to the countryside was perceived to be from spreading urbanisation. The National Trust was formed to buy threatened sites, buildings and areas of particular beauty. By the 20th century, and especially between the wars, the desire of town-dwellers to get out into the countryside for recreation (combined with the improved transport that made this possible) led to clashes between landowners and ramblers. Pressure groups such as the Council for the Preservation of Rural England and the Ramblers' Association were founded at this time.

During the Second World War, the threat to food supplies generated the Dig for Victory campaign, in which people were encouraged to use every available inch of land to grow food. Farming was a key part of the war effort and it was taken for granted that farmers were the best people to safeguard the countryside. State subsidies to farmers were introduced on a massive scale, with a system of price guarantees being introduced in 1947. The intention was to produce more and cheaper food by every means possible.

Developments in agricultural methods since then have been largely the result of this intervention rather than of the free market. This has encouraged the creation of large specialised farming units, involving substantial capital investment. The exception is the special case of small hill-farms where the subsidies have been aimed more at preserving rural communities than producing large amounts of food.

Since the early 1970s, the European Community's Common Agricultural Policy has complicated matters. Its priorities are not those of British policy and an early consequence was the great overproduction of food and the appearance of the notorious butter-mountains and wine-lakes. At the same time, the ecological consequences of some modern intensive farming methods became widely known. From being the guardians of the countryside, farmers became the villains. Overproduction has now led to a reduction in subsidies and the introduction of quotas. Ten million acres is scheduled to be taken out of cultivation in the next few years.

What is to happen to these acres and to the countryside as a whole? The interests of conservationists are at odds with those of farmers. The use of the countryside as a playground for city-dwellers brings excessive wear-and-tear on the very beauty-spots which draw people to them. The wish of rural commuters and second home owners to preserve the 'traditional' village where they have bought property conflicts with the interests of the locals whose livelihood depends on the creation of employment. New motorways provide no direct economic benefit to those who live in the areas they pass through, but are supported by the road lobby.

The politics of the countryside are a key issue of the nineties.

16 MARCH 1990

Discussion Topic

What planning and development policies are needed for the country-side?

FURTHER READING

Newby, H. (1986) *Green and Pleasant Land?* (Wildwood House).
Newby, H. (1988) *The Countryside in Question* (Hutchinson).

Part II
Research

Few students, especially at A level, get the chance to hear practising researchers talking about their work, and so miss out on one of the most stimulating aspects of sociology. The following article is an introduction to social research and to the interviews which follow.

59

Social Research

An Introduction

'Good social science, like all good science, is based on good evidence' (McNeill 1990). That is easy to write, but it is much harder actually to produce good evidence, to demonstrate that it is good, and to draw good conclusions from it.

A skim through a few volumes of sociological research shows what a wide variety of evidence is used by sociologists, and the many different forms a research study can take.

A basic distinction is between quantitative and qualitative data. Quantitative data is statistical, and is usually presented in the form of tables, graphs, bar-charts, pie-charts and the like. It may be simply descriptive, but, if the researcher wants to demonstrate a cause-and-effect relationship, the data will be presented in a way that shows how variables are related to each other.

Such data may be drawn from published sources, such as those of the Central Statistical Office, but much of it is collected by sociological research which uses the survey method, using either a postal questionnaire or a structured interview with a carefully selected sample of people.

Qualitative data is essentially words, very often the actual words used by those being studied. It seeks to show the reader how the researched subjects view their own experience, and to give the reader a chance to 'hear' what they have to say. Data like this is usually collected through face-to-face contact between researcher and those being researched, often in an unstructured interview, which may be part of a study carried out using participant observation.

When the researcher's presence is known to the members of the group or community being studied, interviewing is possible. When the researcher is making the study covertly, all such word-for-word quotations have to be memorised and written down later.

There is a link between the kind of data preferred by a researcher, the methods they use to collect it, and their theoretical assumptions. This link is less clear-cut than it once was, but it is still broadly true that a researcher who relies solely on the use of statistical data will argue that social science should, to some extent, follow the example of research in the natural sciences.

Thus a research project should start with a clear hypothesis that has been devised by the researcher. Data is then collected to test this hypothesis, which is refuted, supported or modified in the light of the data collected. Such research is often trying to explain a social phenomenon.

Those who prefer qualitative data take a less pre-structured approach to their work. Rather than testing a hypothesis or theory, they turn things round and aim to construct theory from the data they collect. The researcher embarks on the data-collection, usually using ethnographic methods, with as open a mind as possible. The published report is essentially descriptive, with theoretical analysis by the researcher in the light of the evidence collected.

In terms of the traditional sociological perspectives, quantitative data is associated with a positivist approach (similar to natural science) and qualitative data with an interpretive approach (concerned with meaning and understanding). Many sociologists, however, would be very happy to see the last of these terms, which have come, at 'A' level at least, to be used far too rigidly. They are useful categories, but are not, and never have been, strictly defined compartments into which any individual sociologist can be placed.

Most researchers use a variety of methods of data-collection, and would strongly resist being categorised as 'positivist' or 'interpretivist', and few research studies fit neatly into these or any other categories.

The methods used in social research make the most of the social skills that we all use in everyday life. We make sense of our surroundings through watching other people (a kind of participant observation); we ask people questions (where the sociologist carries out interviews or distributes questionnaires); we make intelligent guesses about why people are behaving as they do (where the sociologist might develop a hypothesis); we compare one situation with another (a process on which all explanation ultimately depends). Sometimes we even try out some way of behaving to see what the effect is – a kind of experiment.

This link between everyday activities and research techniques makes good social research both easier and more difficult than research in the natural sciences. It is easier because social researchers do not need so much specialised apparatus to do their work, and they are able to communicate directly with their subject-matter if they wish to do so. They can understand what is happening in human terms.

It is more difficult because the researcher has to be so painstakingly careful not to allow personal bias or assumptions to affect the research, and must strive to minimise the impact the research act makes on the behaviour of the people being studied, who will usually know very well that they are being researched. The specialised techniques of social research, while making the most of the fact that the researcher is able to communicate with the subject-matter, also aim to ensure that bias and distortion are reduced to a minimum.

What distinguishes both social and natural science from non-science and from common sense is good method. Good sociology is logically related to valid and reliable empirical evidence. Nothing is taken on trust, but is always subjected to critical analysis in the light of all the evidence available.

23 OCTOBER 1987

Discussion Topic

Think of some social event or aspect of social life that is currently in the news. Make a list of all the ways in which data might be collected about it. Decide which combination of sources would provide the most satisfactory sociological account of the phenomenon you have chosen.

FURTHER READING

McNeill, P. (1990) *Research Methods* (Routledge).
Rose, G. (1982) *Deciphering Sociological Research* (Macmillan).

60

Social Attitudes

The British Attitude Survey

British Social Attitudes, 1987, the third annual report from Social and Community Planning Research, was published at the end of October 1987. Sharon Witherspoon, a member of the research team, was interviewed.

PAT McNEILL: What was the reason for starting this series of annual surveys?

SHARON WITHERSPOON: There is a great deal of factual information about Britain – what people have and do – but there is not much systematic information about feelings, attitudes and beliefs. We wanted to establish regular and impartial monitoring of these, to set alongside the factual information.

PM: Factual data is needed for social policy and planning, but why do we need to know about social attitudes?

SW: First, attitudes are relevant to policy too. For example, it's difficult to make policy about increasing home ownership, without taking account of the fact that some people prefer to rent, for all sorts of reasons. Second, knowledge about attitudes and beliefs is valuable in public debate, where someone may claim to know what people generally think. We can assess whether or not that is true.

PM: Who pays for the research?

SW: About two thirds of funding comes from the Sainsbury family trusts on a three-year rolling basis, which allows us to plan ahead and helps us maintain our impartiality. But we want the data to be used, so about 30 to 40 per cent of funding is from government departments. We jointly agree an area that is relevant to policy concerns and then draft questions. Our core funding helps us to keep final control over questionnaire content.

PM: I understand that the research design involves the use of two separate questionnaires.

SW: Yes. There is a main questionnaire, which is administered face-to-face by a trained interviewer, and there is a self-completion questionnaire. The main questionnaire takes about an hour, with interviewers reading out the questions exactly as they are printed. Respondents mainly take their answers from a set of preselected categories. So there isn't the depth of qualitative interviewing, but you do have large numbers of answers to exactly the same question. There are also a few open ended questions. These are much more difficult to analyse, but they can be crucial in giving background information.

The second questionnaire is for self-completion and takes about 20 minutes. It deals with simpler information, and has to be clearly designed, carefully worded, and very easy to read.

PM: What kind of response rate do you get?

SW: Overall, about 70 per cent of the people we approach complete the interview questionnaire. This is lower than we might like, but it is a reasonably good response rate nowadays. Then about 90 per cent of those return the self-completion questionnaire. People who don't respond are slightly more likely to be the very old or the very young, and many are just very busy at the time.

PM: How do you pilot the questionnaires?

SW: We often start with qualitative interviews. We research an issue, and then special interviewers discuss these topics in depth with a few people. This gives us an idea of the language people actually use and what aspects are important to them. We draft questions, and the pilot surveys are conducted with between 25 and 100 respondents.

PM: What are the difficulties?

SW: There can be problems with the topic. For example, the 1987 survey asked about attitudes to and perceptions of AIDS. We piloted this several times before we felt satisfied that the language we used was both neutral and understandable.

Another kind of difficulty is more technical. We use 'filtered' questions, questions that are only asked if certain answers have previously been given. We have to pilot these to make the interview flow smoothly. And sometimes questions just don't work.

PM: What is your sampling procedure?

SW: Details are in the book, but essentially it is a multi-stage random sampling design. The first stage is to select a number of parliamentary constituencies; then we select one polling district from each constituency. Next, using the electoral register, we select specific households. Finally, from each household, we select one individual to be interviewed. At every stage, we use random procedures to ensure representativeness.

PM: Are the results collated by computer?

SW: Yes, but we also use clerical editing. The coders go through each questionnaire checking for unanswered questions and correct filtering; they also code open-ended questions and look at notes made by interviewers. The data is then analysed by computer. It is programmed to check for logical consistency and completeness. But computers can never fully substitute for human judgement.

PM: My last question concerns the issue of validity. How do you know whether you are collecting evidence about people's real attitudes, or about what people will say when they are asked what their attitude is?

SW: This is the hardest question of all. First, we look for consistency. We try never to have a single measure of any topic. For example, on nationalisation, we have questions about state ownership and about attitudes to particular nationalised industries. The questions are of different types and may be in different parts of the questionnaire.

Second, we ask interviewers to annotate the questionnaires, including their assessment of whether respondents understood and cared about the questions. We routinely ask interviewers which questions were difficult for respondents.

Third, we look for correlations which we know from past experience should be there. So, for example, we expect nationalisation to correlate with party political views. If the correlations are odd or weak, then we suspect the validity of the responses.

A qualitative researcher doing a depth interview can really probe, whereas we are much more distant from our respondents. But the qualitative researcher can say little about representativeness or correlations. If you want representativeness, you have to have numbers and distance. So we have to be on the alert for our own mistakes, and we try to be open about them. We say 'Despite our pilot of 50 interviews, when we did 3000 this question didn't work'. This sense of scepticism keeps quantitative research on its toes.

18 NOVEMBER 1987

Discussion Topic

If you are carrying out a survey as part of your course, what are the important practical points to be learned from this interview?

61

Researching Child Abuse

Ethnographic Techniques

PAT McNEILL: What is the subject of your research?

STEVE TAYLOR:* I'm researching child abuse, and in particular how various experts, such as social workers and doctors, come to 'recognise' that a child has been abused or is 'at risk'.

PM: Is your work intended to guide social policy in this area?

ST: As a sociologist, what concerns me is that most people researching this area oversimplify the problem. They assume that there is a thing called child abuse which is relatively easy to define, that it happens, and that it is easy to identify who is being abused. For them, the only questions are about why it happens.

I think the sociologist has to say: 'Before we get into those questions we must see what we mean by child abuse, what officials mean by child abuse and how we respond to what we perceive to be child abuse'. Then you can say to social workers, doctors and others:

These are the theories you are implicitly working with when you define one case as child abuse and another as normal parenting. What do you think of these theories? Do you want to go back and re-examine them? Do you think you should be doing anything differently?

This type of research can help practitioners to clarify their thinking and improve the quality of their work.

PM: What research methods are you using?

ST: First, we did formal interviews with the various professional groups involved. We asked them how they defined child abuse, and how they recognised something as a case of child abuse. But sociologists should not just reproduce what people say, and you cannot conduct research purely on interviews. So, having identified some of the things professionals saw as problematic about child abuse, we did some participant observation. This meant going out with social workers on visits, going to case conferences and to court in order to see their ideas in action.

At the same time, we were able to put further questions; for example, asking social workers to explain particular decisions. We also used documentary data, such as social work files and case conference minutes.

We formed the impression during the research that social services felt under such pressure from the media, from policy guidelines and from lack of resources that they were being more defensive and were bringing more cases to court than they really wished to, or would have done a few years earlier. Official figures show that the proportion of children coming into care compulsorily has increased in the last few years. Some people suggest that this is because the abuse is on the increase. Our data suggests that it can be explained by our changing response to children at risk.

At one point I played the role of a trainee social worker. The advantage of this was that I could be more sure that people weren't being extra efficient and careful for my benefit. The disadvantage was that I couldn't stop people and ask them research questions. It's not a question of a right or wrong method. You pick your method to suit the nature of the problem, and you look for interplay between methods.

PM: Is it difficult to keep your own personal values distinct from the research you are doing?

ST: If we let our personal values predominate, then we cease to be sociologists. Just recently, every politician and pundit has suddenly become an expert on child abuse. If you are on the political right, it's because of the decline in family values. If you are left of centre, it's because of bad housing, stress, and the deprivations of capitalism. If you are into feminism, it's just another example of male power.

All these views are immediate political responses, and there is an important distinction between politics and sociology. Politicians only look for evidence to confirm a preconceived view. Sociology, on the other hand, is about discovery. The sociologist may have preconceived views, but research must be structured so that there is always the chance of discovering the unexpected.

You must also keep your emotions as well as your values out of research. As a citizen, child abuse alarms me. As a social scientist, it is behaviour to be observed and analysed.

PM: What other concepts have you developed during the research?

ST: The purpose of a concept is to help clarify and analyse the mass of data that you are working with. Our key concept was the 'danger cue'. This means any piece of evidence which alerts a professional worker to a possible case of child abuse. An obvious example would be a child with severe physical injuries. But there are many other things that worry the professionals, but have nothing to do with the physical condition of the child; the background, the state of the home, the nature of the family.

From this observation we made a distinction between primary and secondary danger cues. Primary cues were those which related to the condition of the child; physical injury, anal bleeding, something like that. Secondary cues were those which related to something other than the child's condition; social class, racial origin, whether the parents had been abused as children, the nature of the family, the way the parents talked and so on.

As you move through the list you find that it is increasingly subjective, and we found that many decisions were made which had less to do with the condition of the child than with the nature of the family. So from this distinction we were able to conclude that many decisions about children at risk are taken on the basis of how families are living their lives, explaining their actions and so on.

Professionals have assumptions about the kind of people who do and don't harm their children, and it takes very strong evidence to contradict those assumptions.

In short, professionals theorise about child abuse, and these theories structure their perception of the problem. I think distinguishing between the two types of cue illustrated this in a way that would not otherwise have been so clear.

15 JANUARY 1988

Discussion Topic

Like all social research, this must be critically evaluated.
How valid do you think Taylor's data is likely to be? How reliable is it?

* Steve Taylor lectures at the London School of Economics.

62

Community Studies

Researching a Scottish Community

PAT McNEILL: What is your research about?

GEOFF PAYNE:* We are making a community study of a crofting area on the west coast of Scotland. It has a population of about three hundred.

PM: How did you come to choose this area of study?

GP: Whatever the textbooks say about how research is designed, there are all sorts of quirky reasons for doing a particular piece of work. I'd been visiting the area on holiday for several years, and then I took a short lease on a cottage. I became interested, and then met Angus Macleod who is a native of the area and made a study of it for his undergraduate dissertation.

PM: So you have effectively bypassed the standard issues of making contact with the community, the key informant, and so on?

ANGUS MACLEOD:* Yes. And, in addition, the test census for 1991 was done in the area, so we can use this secondary data to make a study of things like age structure and family structure.

PM: What stage have you reached?

GP: The first stage in research is planning. You can't just go in and start looking, nor can you study the whole of social life. So we are discussing methods and identifying issues we wish to study.

PM: Isn't there a danger that, knowing the area so well, you will make assumptions about what you are going to find?

GP: Well, yes and no. Although Angus has a lot of prior knowledge, I don't, so I have been piecing together a picture of life in the area which is based on key informants and a kind of snowballing approach. I have been doing this informally, while on holiday, since about 1985. I've been doing some very unsystematic observation, listening to talk in the pub and so on.

PM: When you start systematic data-collection, will you let it be known that you are doing research? Hitherto, effectively, you have been covert. Does anybody in the community know what you are about?

AM: Yes, they know that we are studying the community. Many of them think we are interested in the social history. I've actively played that up, because I think people have a common-sense idea of what history is, whereas sociology is more alien. We have also used a portable video camera. People get used to us taking pictures, and it is a useful observational tool.

GP: It's particularly useful for shots of group activity. For example, a number of women had a coffee morning in the village hall and raised funds for the local school. I was able to wander about filming individuals and groups over a two-hour period. Later, I showed it to Angus and asked, 'Who's the lady with the white hair?' or 'Who's this guy?' It makes an excellent record.

It's important to recognise that a video-recording is an artefact. You are making a film, and editing it. Sociologists deal with words all the time and we tend to forget that, when writing, we are doing something artefactual. But with video I am conscious of making choices all the time. Do I include this shot or that shot? And why? The video camera brings out the fact that you are generating or creating evidence as much as you are collecting it.

But it is an immensely powerful medium, and people have a tendency to think: 'If it's on TV it must be true'. We have to be very careful how we use it, and stress that people should not take the material at face-value. We have a whole new source of data here available to sociologists and we don't yet know how to use it.

PM: In the next phase of research, will one of you take up residence?

AM: Yes, I'll be there from Easter until Christmas.

PM: Will that be participant observation in its classic sense? Given your links with the area, there are roles already there for you, like cousin or old schoolfriend. Do you expect that to create any difficulties?

AM: I suppose people may be scared to tell me too much, but they also tend not to take me seriously. 'Young Angus thinks he is a researcher!' Obviously, I have to fit into my basic roles, like being a young male and a member of my family.

GP: On the other hand, some people have said to me, when they heard Angus was going to do it, 'Well, that's all right then'. He's one of their own.

PM: Obviously, the concept of community is itself problematic, but are there any other concepts that you have identified as important to your study?

GP: Yes, the related concepts of local, incomer, outsider and settler have very subtle meanings. My landlord only uses his house as a holiday home, so he is not a settler. My immediate neighbour is another English incomer who is a settler.

AM: There are degrees of localness and degrees of incomers, and the distinction between the two can change quickly and radically. A visiting folk-singer got drunk and broke the windows of the hotel-manager's car. Now, the hotel manager is very unpopular. He's an incomer though he's been there for nearly 20 years. But local people were angry that this folk-singer had smashed one of *our* cars. They redrew the boundaries overnight; for a few days, anyway.

GP: There is also a class dimension. There are some people who are fairly recent incomers who are Scottish and working class. They just mix in and it would take a little while to know they weren't long-term residents.

PM: This is a study of a very small group of people. What is its value?

AM: It has been said that the anthropology of ourselves is still a dream. We still don't know enough about our neighbour and his habits. This is just a little slice of life, but we can get it on record. So the first reason is just a simple descriptive ethnography.

GP: In the Highlands, the life of the communities is changing but it is also being sustained. It isn't all decay and the loss of a romantic way of life. The village schools are full of young children; the economy is being buoyed up, partly by tourism; more roads are being opened up; it's being sustained through investment by international capital. So the research is saying something about change.

I don't have any illusions that this is a microcosm of British society, or the 'typical' community. There are aspects of it which will be common to other rural communities, and aspects which are common but with a local variation. Community studies are like small chips being put on thinly to build a whole. But that is a legitimate thing to do.

4 MARCH 1988

* Geoff Payne and Angus Macleod are both from Plymouth Polytechnic.

63

Documents of Life

Life Histories

PAT McNEILL: Social research is often associated only with social surveys, and possibly with ethnography. But your book is about 'documents of life'. What are they?

KEN PLUMMER:* They are documents which focus on people's subjective understanding of their own social world. There is a distinction between the naturalistic documents of life, which people produce anyway, like diaries, autobiographies, photographs, even raw videos, and life-histories which are coaxed out by the sociologist, who loosely guides the respondent, asking questions with a specifically sociological slant.

PM: The book is subtitled *A Humanistic Method*. What is the significance of that?

KP: It's to do with the distinction between the humanities and the sciences. Humanistic sociology is scientific in the sense that it is disciplined, critical and systematic, but it has more in common with the arts than with the natural sciences, with feeling your way around a subject, with being sensitive to the variation of social life rather than looking for abstract generalisations. It assumes that people are active and creative in the world.

Of course, sociology must look at structures, but what humanistic sociology does is to show that human beings constantly resist those structures, they fight back, they have alternative views, and, although they are constrained, they are constantly doing things in the world. It is very important that students appreciate structures and constraints, because that is not the conventional way of thinking about social life. But once you have grasped that, then you have to temper it with the fact that people aren't puppets.

PM: When did sociologists first use this sort of material?

KP: It is generally considered to be Thomas and Znaniecki *The Polish*

Peasant published in 1918. For 20 years it was regarded in American sociology as the best and most perfect example of sociology. And then by the late 1940s no one ever mentioned it. Most students never hear of it today.

PM: Why did that happen?

KP: From the 1940s, American sociology became either very abstractly theoretical, as in the work of Parsons, or highly methodologically sophisticated, as with Paul Lazarsfeld. In the 1960s there was a resurgence of interest in interactionism, largely through the work of Howard Becker. The book that brought life-history back into focus was *The Jack-Roller*, the story of Stanley, a mugger as he'd now be called, written by Clifford Shaw and first published in 1925. Becker wrote the introduction to the revised 1966 edition, and spelled out the sociological value of the life-history.

PM: Has the method any potential for the A level student doing a project?

KP: Oh, yes. The most obvious use is to open up an area of inquiry that is new to you. Often students say, 'I'll construct a questionnaire and then go and ask a few people'. But the better way is to find a key informant, someone who knows a lot about it, and to get right into their lives, probe them as deeply as possible, try to come to understand how they see the world. Use that as the basis for getting lots of ideas into your head, lots of questions about how you want to proceed. That's just as valuable for the professional researcher.

It's much better to have one or two people who know what they are talking about than 100 who don't. Look at photographs, and read letters, or just go and walk about the places people live and work in. Start with the individual and work out to the structure.

PM: Having done that, what choices are open?

KP: Life-history can be seen either as a *resource* or as a *topic* for study. To use life-history as a resource is to look, for instance, at a delinquent's life-story and to try to set it into the already existing sociological theories. You might decide that it doesn't fit them. Then you can go beyond present theory and develop new ideas. That's viewing it as a resource, and is probably the best way for students. But it is also possible, although harder, to treat life-history as a topic, and to analyse how and why people come to tell stories of their lives, to view social life as a process of story-telling.

PM: What are the problems of researching life-histories?

KP: The main problem is that it is time-consuming and hard work. It's said that the main weaknesses are the lack of representativeness and of validity. I don't see representativeness as a problem, because any life-history is always representative of a larger group. It will always tell you something about more than that one person. Validity is a more serious problem because you don't know if somebody is telling the truth. There could be lies, fronts put on, loss of memory. But if that's true of a life-history, which you painstakingly gather over ten or 15 hours, how much more true is it of a ten-minute interview?

PM: What about the questions of bias and objectivity?

KP: This is a very complex area. The basic point is that truth is always situated in a context, and you have to take that context into account. If you try to remove all sources of bias, the interviewer just sits there doing nothing, and that in itself is a bias, because the person being interviewed won't like it. The sociologist has to make the context of the research explicit, and the reader has to judge the value of the research in that context.

PM: What are the ethical issues in life-history research?

KP: One is the personal entanglement you can get with someone, because you are not just seeing them once for half an hour, you're spending a long time with them. But the big issue is that you are using them, and that is potentially exploitation. Why should anybody talk to a social researcher? Again, this is an issue in all research, but it is particularly acute in getting life-histories.

In addition, there are the ever-present issues of anonymity and confidentiality. You can lose somebody in a sample of 2000, but however much you change details of names and places in a life-history, somebody is going to recognise who it is.

20 MAY 1988

FURTHER READING

Becker, H. (1978) 'The Life History', in P. Worsley *Modern Sociology* (Penguin).

Plummer, K. (1982) *Documents of Life* (George Allen & Unwin, reissued 1990 by Unwin/Hyman).

* Ken Plummer lectures at the University of Essex.

64

Researching in Schools

> *Life in Classrooms*

PAT McNEILL: You have published a great deal of work based on your research in schools, often using the technique of non-participant observation. What does this involve?

PETER WOODS:* It is important not to exaggerate the difference between participant observation and non-participant observation. As a participant observer, you undertake a role within a group or institution. In the case of a school, for example, you might do some teaching so that you can understand better the mental processes, perspectives and problems faced by a person occupying that role. In non-participant observation, you observe a situation from a detached position which doesn't intrude nor take over any of the roles of the people interacting in that situation. A term often used is a 'fly on the wall'. The problem with this model is that observers are not flies and, with schools in particular, the observer inevitably influences the interaction to some degree. The non-participant observer doesn't deliberately undertake a role, but may be forced into one. For example, I have recently been researching in primary schools observing a class of 7-year-olds. It is impossible to sit in a class of 7-year-olds and not be drawn into their interaction. Young children will respond to you as a teacher, as an adult, as a parent. They are very forthcoming, totally uninhibited, they like having someone else there. They drag you in. It would be counter-productive to the research to resist this. The only way of doing it would be to look through a spyhole, and that's ethically dubious.

PM: But aren't teachers uncomfortable about having an outsider in their classroom?

PW: Yes, and that is entirely understandable. But the effect depends on how you go about it. You have to develop a code of ethics and a feeling of mutual trust at an early stage. You have to remove the sense of threat you bring to the situation, the sort of threat that might be felt from inspectors or advisers. You have to reassure them about the purposes of your research, the means you will employ and the uses to which the research will be put. I've never come across a teacher who didn't respond to something which they felt was genuinely in the interests of education. You must convince them of that, and of your credentials as an educational researcher, and provide them with the guarantee of confidentiality.

PM: How does the presence of the researcher affect the children?

PW: That varies by age. I've already referred to what happens with younger children, and how they involve you in their interaction. Older students, by the time they are fourteen or fifteen, don't intrude in the same way as 7-year-olds when you are observing a classroom, but in other settings they will talk to you about their perspectives and ideas. Occasionally in the classroom they may draw your attention to some aspect of the interaction that illustrates a point they have made outside. All of this is interesting and usable material.

PM: So it is possible, with experience, to become confident that the account you are giving is a valid one.

PW: You hope so. This is where the qualitative method scores very highly. You are trying to understand what is going on in this particular piece of interaction, what are the underlying rules of behaviour in it. These may not be the same as the manifest rules. They may have been developed over a long period, through subtle forms of negotiation that people are not able to articulate but which an observer can extrapolate from the situation. One of the virtues of observation is that it takes place over a long period of time, which enables you to develop a good relationship with people. It's very difficult for someone to sustain a front for so long, so they relax and are themselves, and you can observe the full range of activities and experiences that go on within that group. You use a range of techniques to get at this. You observe at different times of the day; you talk to them in different situations, at the school, in the playground, in their home, in yours, in the pub. You look at documentation. You attend staff meetings. You begin to perceive themes in what is happening, and you focus on these areas. You seek to support or discard them, using comparative data from your other observations.

PM: Isn't this research just rediscovering what pupils and teachers already know about what is happening in schools?

PW: Some of it may be, inevitably, since the method seeks to represent their knowledge, perspectives and cultures as faithfully as possible. But the research may also present material of which they are only partly conscious, or not conscious at all, or know only in hazy terms. Because they are so involved in the action they cannot have such a detached view of the whole institution as a non-participant observer, nor can they spend the time collecting material from many different sources, which, when analysed, might cast new light on teaching and learning situations. But they none the less recognise it when it is shown to them.

PM: So you would hope that, when you show your accounts to teachers and pupils, they would say, 'Oh, yes. I recognise that'.

PW: That's right. They know it, but maybe they haven't been able to articulate it before. So you present them with a form of words, and they may say, 'That's it; that's right'.

PM: And what if they say, 'That's not quite right'.

PW: Or even, 'That's totally wrong!' It depends what their motives are, what it is they are talking about, and what other observations and evidence you have about them and about others. But it's all part of the data and it goes into your analysis. Respondent validation, as it's called, is useful but it can have dangers. If you take it to its extremes, you end up with teachers presenting the final conclusions of the research. What has happened then is that the researcher has gone native. There's a polarity between two requirements: observers need to empathise and to associate intimately with the thoughts and actions of the people they are researching, and at the same time they must perceive things more objectively, and perhaps more critically. That's an abiding problem and you have to keep the two in balance. Your degree of involvement and detachment varies from day to day and from week to week. It's not a fixed position.

24 JUNE 1988

Discussion Topic

What might a 'fly on the wall' observe in your sociology classroom?

FURTHER READING

Woods, P. (1986) *Inside Schools: Ethnography in Educational Research* (RKP).

---

* Peter Woods is a professor at the Open University.

65

A Chronicle of Crime

The British Crime Survey

PAT McNEILL: The British Crime Survey was set up in 1982 to investigate crime through a sample survey which asks people about their experience of crime. What prompted its establishment?

PAT MAYHEW (Principal Research Officer at the Home Office Research and Planning Unit): It is recognised that the official statistics of crime have their limitations. There were already established victim surveys in the USA (since 1972), in Canada, and in Australia. There was growing concern about crime, and the summer of 1981 was that of the riots. There was a need for more information, and victim surveys give a more rounded picture than police statistics. BCSs have been published in 1983 and 1985 and the third will appear in 1989. The more surveys you do, the more useful the data becomes, because it is then possible to analyse trends. This is valuable data for the Home Office, which funds the research.

PMcN: What is the design of the survey?

PM: Many forms of crime are rare, so we have to have a big sample, about 11,000 households. In 1982 the only feasible sampling frame was the electoral register. Today, PAF (the Post Office Address File) is a better frame and in 1988 we thought about whether to switch to it. But we found that this might mean a loss of comparability. Anything that jeopardises comparability over the years, like changing the interviewing period, or going over to PAF, has consequences which cannot be precisely quantified. So in the end we decided to stick with the electoral register.

PMcN: How satisfied are you with the sample?

PM: I have checked the 1988 sample by matching it against OPCS data in terms of age and sex distribution, and it is really quite good. But the sample doesn't cover people in institutions, who may be disproportionately victimised. There is an ethnic minority 'booster sample' in the 1988 survey but there are no population statistics available to check its representativeness. From the sample, one person aged over 16 per household is interviewed face-to-face, at their own address, with a standardised questionnaire. The interview can last from 25 minutes to over an hour. The response rate is nearly 80 per cent, which is very good.

PMcN: How do you draft the questions?

PM: In drafting the questions and in designing the structure of the questionnaire we learned a lot from the earlier surveys. For example, we use 'screener' questions. If you ask people whether they have been a victim of a particular crime and, when they say 'yes', you immediately ask for details, they quickly learn that to say 'yes' means that they will have more questions to answer. So you ask about all the possible crimes in a list. If they say 'yes' to any of the crimes, only at the end do you question further.

We also had difficulty in drafting questions to measure the fear of crime, so that we can compare it with the actual crime rate in the area. That has been difficult, but we have collected some useful data.

Most countries have a fixed questionnaire, but we went for a fixed core with a system of optional components, so we can change topics from one survey to another. For instance, the 1988 survey has a component on contacts with the police. This is a valuable feature for funders. The actual survey is carried out by survey companies.

PMcN: Are you aware of any particular weak areas in the data?

PM: Yes, the measurement of domestic abuse and of sexual assault, because of the problem of respondents being too reticent to answer frankly. Our first attempt didn't work well, but we changed the wording of the question. The rate of reported sexual assault actually doubled, though from a very small base. The interview also covers some self-reported offences, because we wanted to investigate the overlap between victims and offenders, the largest group in both cases being young males.

People were sceptical about whether respondents would co-operate, but this itself was not a problem, though respondents may none the less have concealed offences. We gave respondents a pack of cards, each with an offence on it, from which they had to select which offences they had committed. Respondents enjoyed it, and many asked to have a pack for their Christmas party! When we analysed the 1982 data, we found very low admission rates. So we changed the procedure in 1984, and asked first 'How many people do you think did this?'. When they had said, for instance, that most people fiddled their income tax returns, it was much easier for them to admit it.

PMcN: How is the BCS published?

PM: There is the main report published by HMSO, but there are also many other publications, including many journal articles. It's not just a single book, but a continuous flow of material.

PMcN: What is the police response?

PM: Quite good. The BCS data is too dispersed to say anything about local conditions, but various police forces have set up local surveys. They are usually simpler than BCS, but the idea is the same. The police seem to have a positive perception of victim surveys.

PMcN: Since it finds much higher crime rates than the official statistics, doesn't the BCS actually make people more fearful?

PM: The point of the survey is to show crime as it really is, and the truth is that a great number of crimes are relatively trivial property ones, despite what people imagine and what the media suggest. An important finding is that the risk to the elderly of being assaulted is low. This is not explained by their staying in, which is the usual retort. We matched elderly people who did go out with other age groups and found that they are still not as vulnerable as younger people.

Similarly, we have shown, like the American survey, that the upward trend of crime is slower than police statistics show.

It seems that some of the increase in police figures is to do with more reporting to the police and possibly more recording.

9 DECEMBER 1988

Discussion Topic

Make a content analysis of property crime reported in the national press during one week, and another of property crime reported in your local paper over the same period. How would you account for the differences you find?

FURTHER READING

Hough, M. and Mayhew, P. (1983) *B.C.S. First Report* (HMSO).
Hough, M. and Mayhew, P. (1985) *Taking Account of Crime* (HMSO).

66

Moonie Myths

Values and Value-relevance

PAT MCNEILL: Dr Barker, you are best known to A level sociologists for your book *The Making of a Moonie* (Blackwell, 1984), in which you asked the question 'Why should – how could – anyone become a Moonie?' Many people assume that Moonie converts must have been 'brainwashed', but you found that 90 per cent of those who go to the residential Moonie workshops don't become Moonies, and that most who join the Unification Church leave of their own freewill within two years. Your very thorough research led you to conclude that the 'brainwashing' wasn't very effective. You got excellent academic reviews, and a special book award for your methodological approach, but how was it received by the Moonies?

EILEEN BARKER:* Most of them considered it irrelevant. A few said it was helpful to see themselves through the eyes of an outsider. Others thought I'd betrayed them because I should have presented their point of view rather than addressing sociological questions.

PM: What was the reaction of the anti-cultists, who make it their task to oppose religious cults? Wasn't your book a challenge to their position and a threat to their interests?

EB: Again, reactions varied. One or two said the book changed their perspective, but the more virulent anti-cultists have been very hostile, especially those who are directly or indirectly involved in deprogramming, which is the practice of kidnapping people in an attempt to 'rescue' them from the movements. Parents are persuaded to pay deprogrammers thousands of pounds to carry out this illegal act, after being told that this is the only way in which they are likely to get their child back (the child may be 30 years old).

Obviously deprogrammers aren't too keen on research which shows that it isn't true that people can't leave the cults of their own free will, that deprogramming often doesn't work, and that, even when it does 'succeed', it can create severe problems for the people concerned.

As no one has managed to refute my findings (other scholars have produced very similar results), the best the anti-cultists can do is to launch a personal attack saying, for example, that because I'm an academic I don't care about parents' anguish. Some even accuse me of being a Moonie. Despite the fact that I have written things that the movements themselves consider highly critical of their practices, my refusal to proclaim that everything about all cults is totally evil is taken as proof that I must be 'pro-cult'. This is understandable if one recognises that anti-cultists, like some of the cults they attack, often want everything presented in terms of a simple good-or-bad divide.

PM: It's clear that your knowledge of the 'cult scene' has engendered strong feelings in you. This had led to your establishing INFORM, the Information Network Focus on Religious Movements. Can you tell me about that?

EB: Well, I found myself observing an enormous amount of what I considered unnecessary suffering. Frequently this was because some movements, some anti-cultists and some of the media had given parents unreliable information that caused them acute anxiety and/or obscured genuine difficulties. Eventually, I decided something more than note-taking needed to be done and, with the support of the mainstream Churches, the British Sociological Association and the British Association for Counselling, and with funding from the Home Office, INFORM came into being last year.

It tries to help people by providing information that's as objective and up-to-date as possible; it alerts people to problems that may be encountered in some of the movements; and it can put enquirers in touch with a growing network of specialists and counsellors. It also runs seminars to inform clergy and counsellors about the effects that new religions can have on people.

PM: You have always stressed the importance of social science being as objective as possible, yet you are clearly taking up an evaluative position by establishing INFORM, and by writing your latest book *New Religious Movements: A Practical Introduction* (HMSO, 1989).

EB: Yes, but I don't see my position as at all contradictory. On the contrary, it seems silly to think objective, value-free research is value-less. It strikes me that it's the most valuable kind of research. It is a value-judgment that social science ought to be as free as possible of the researcher's values, and, of course, it's pretty well impossible to be completely value-free. But I can't see much point in the kind of sociology where the reader learns more about the researcher's values than about the phenomenon itself.

When I decided to explore the brainwashing thesis, this was partly because I thought if Moonies do use successful brainwashing techniques, then something ought to be done about it by people other than deprogrammers. If, however, Moonies aren't brainwashed but really want to be Moonies, then they ought to be allowed to live with their choice – so long as they don't harm others or break the law. When I decided to set up INFORM, it was because I believed people who have important decisions to make about how, for example, to react to a relative or friend joining a new religious movement, ought to have access to the carefully researched information that social scientists are producing.

Social science can't do everything; it can't decide, for example, between theological and other non-empirical claims, and it can't tell people what is right or wrong, or tell them what to do. What it can do is to help them towards an accurate understanding of the situation they have to deal with and alert them to some of the possible consequences of their actions.

Those of us involved in INFORM believe in truth and in respect for the individual. We believe that objective knowledge is superior to uninformed bigotry. We don't believe (as some of the cults and the anti-cultists seem to believe) that one can wave a magic wand to get rid of all the world's problems. But we have been able to help lots of people. Academic research need not be irrelevant to the practical problems that people face.

7 JULY 1989

Discussion Topic

'Value-free; value-less; value-relevant'. Can you clarify the differences between them?

* Eileen Barker lectures at the London School of Economics.

67

Ask Nicely

The Ethics of Social Research

Many of my students are alert to the issue of cruelty to laboratory animals. They can argue a good case against their use in research concerned only to develop cosmetics, or to find out things that can be discovered in other ways. Some argue the most difficult case, that animals should not even be used in research which clearly saves human lives.

But they often seem rather less concerned when questions of morality are raised in connection with sociological research. With the rapid increase in courses which require students to conduct their own research, some of these ethical issues are of immediate practical relevance.

First, there is the question of when or whether it is justifiable to collect social data at all. Researchers should consider what benefits might follow and for whom, what harm might be done and to whom, and where the balance lies. Even when the anonymity of respondents is guaranteed to prevent their exposure to ridicule or even punitive action, harm may come from the process of collection. A student's proposal that she would interview a sample of women about the experience of having a baby die in the first year of life was unacceptable on these grounds.

On the other hand, it may be possible to show that the outcome of an enquiry might benefit those researched, as in a survey of demand for a new youth centre or sports facility. This would help justify the project. Similarly, social researchers sometimes claim that they can provide those whose views are usually ignored with a chance to put their case.

The argument that respondents can choose whether to co-operate in research, especially survey-based projects, is not necessarily a good one. All such research trades to some extent on the goodwill of those approached. Some people may find it more difficult to refuse a youngster who explains that the survey is an essential part of their coursework than a professional researcher. This is even more the case where the student is a relative, a friend or a neighbour.

Consent is particularly important when the subjects of the research are lonely, powerless or both. A lonely person may welcome the opportunity to talk to anyone who seems interested, but once the interview is over, who has gained more? Powerless people, such as those who rely on state benefits, are all too used to having to answer personal questions. Should they be asked to answer more?

These questions have been addressed in recent years, particularly by women researchers who are investigating women's lives. Janet Finch (1984), for example, was at first surprised at how readily her respondents answered her questions. On reflection, she concluded that women are more used to answering questions from officials, that an informal interview conducted by a female researcher in another woman's home comes to resemble an intimate conversation between equals, and that many lonely women welcomed the opportunity to discuss their lives with a sympathetic listener.

Finch is concerned that the trust a woman interviewer can establish with a woman interviewee may be open to exploitation. One way of reducing the risk is to approach the interviewee as an equal, but this has the ironic result of producing even more private information.

Research done largely through observation, participant or not, raises further ethical issues. First, should a researcher act in an overt or covert manner? Can researching people without their knowledge ever be justified? Where data-collection depends on observing groups of anonymous and unknown people, such as a football crowd, there is perhaps no great problem. Where the researcher participates in the group in any way, matters are different. Knowing an observer was present could well distort people's behaviour so much as to make any observations worthless, but this may be a reason to abandon the enquiry rather than to proceed secretly.

And from whom should permission for the research be sought? In the case of an institutional study there is a tendency to ask the authority figure, such as a head-teacher or an officer-in-charge. Perhaps the children or residents should be asked whether they consent to having their daily lives observed and recorded by someone whose major motive is not to improve their lot, but to pass an examination.

In this kind of small-scale research, it is harder to preserve anonymity and to protect confidentiality. In a survey, individuals can be 'lost' in statistics, but in ethnography the individuals speak to us through the researcher.

The British Sociological Association's Code of Ethical Principles advocates the principle of 'informed consent' when carrying out social research. It argues that researchers should explain the reasons for their project and the implications for individual subjects or groups and communities. Subjects should understand that they have the right to refuse to co-operate. They should be told where and when the results of the research will be available. Obviously, researchers should never lie to their subjects, but there is a great temptation to be economical with the truth. They should also beware that some authority figures will assume that the researcher is 'on their side' and will keep them informed of everything that happens.

Like all researchers, students also have a responsibility to sociology as a discipline. They should do nothing to bring social research into disrepute or that might make it difficult for others to carry out future work. Bosk (1979) states that researchers should never forget that 'the right and the privilege of being an observer is a gift presented to the researcher by his [*sic*] host and subjects'. This emphasis on the obligations of the gift relationship is right, but the receiver also has a duty to ensure that the gift is given knowingly and willingly.

9 FEBRUARY 1990

Discussion Topic

What kinds of research should be banned on ethical grounds?

FURTHER READING

Bosk, C. (1979) *Forgive and Remember: Managing Medical Failure* (Chicago).

Finch, J. (1984) '"It's great to have someone to talk to": the ethics and politics of interviewing women', in C. Bell and H. Roberts, *Social Researching* (RKP).

Part III
Sociology

68

Bias in Sociology

| Is Sociology Left-wing? |

The accusation that sociology has a left-wing bias usually comes from outside the discipline, but during 1987 Professor David Marsland joined the right-wing critics.

PAT McNEILL: In your book *Bias against Business*, you argue that introductory sociology, at all levels, is biased against business and against capitalism. Where do you think this bias occurs?

DAVID MARSLAND:* In the first place, there is bias in the way textbook authors select their material, giving one set of approaches and arguments and omitting others. In the second place, some of the texts *seem* to show two sides of a question but, in fact, set up one side so weakly that it is easy to criticise it.

PM: Isn't it the business of sociology to ask awkward questions and to be critical?

DM: We've exaggerated the importance of criticism. We have lost sight of simpler objectives like description and explanation. Of course, there must also be criticism and evaluation, but all these elements are equally important. In any case, even if we accept that criticism is one objective of sociology, the objects of criticism should not be so one-sidedly selected. In the texts I have looked at, coherent criticism of the trade unions, the welfare state, indeed the whole collectivist value system, is very slender. If we really believed in being critical, then we'd be critical of those as much as we criticise individualism and capitalism. We must also have self-criticism, if not, sociology becomes detached from scholarship.

PM: Isn't any selection inevitably biased? Aren't you just saying that your bias is better than my bias?

DM: It's not as easy as that. Take an example: advertising is an enormously important feature of our lives. Yet it is either neglected or dismissed as really rather unpleasant in almost every text. This cannot be plausibly explained in terms of having too many other important things to cover.

PM: In your book, you also refer to Soviet Russia.

DM: Yes, I was honestly surprised at the way that the USSR was treated. There is very little coherent criticism of state socialism in the USSR.

PM: Isn't this just the result of a lack of material that teachers and writers of textbooks can use?

DM: In the case of socialism, absolutely not. There is a large body of ignored material. You can't do scholarly work unless you look at the alternative arguments.

PM: Your whole argument suggests that you believe that it is possible to achieve balance.

DM: Yes. It's a moving equilibrium, of course, but it can be achieved. At the moment the imbalance is morally and educationally wrong. I'd put it stronger than balance. There should be competition, and you can't have competition unless the competitors are somewhere near equal in their access to resources.

PM: Some teachers would argue that it is enough to state your position and to leave the student to take it into account.

DM: It's not enough. Teachers must not only be honest about their own perspectives, but should strive to draw students' attention to all the relevant arguments even if the teacher believes some have major weaknesses. Scholarship requires that due attention is paid to balance, that the weaknesses in one's own argument are emphasised, and that relevant arguments and other evidence are brought to bear. I know it sounds boring, but that's just the bottom line of teaching. Many sociology students say that they just find out what the teacher wants, and give it to them. That's against any definition of education or of scholarship. At grammar school, I was taught to think things through, and express what I thought. Sociology, like classics, should be about enlightenment.

PM: But can't students resist bias, if it is there?

DM: That view underestimates the influence a teacher has. In any case, even if the student can handle bias, such teaching is still bad scholarship.

PM: What do you think of the argument that, since other subjects are so biased, it's up to sociology to restore the overall balance in the curriculum?

DM: There's no real evidence that politics or economics are biased in the other direction. The people who use the argument are obviously not convinced of it themselves because they usually throw in other influences like the media and the whole structure of society. Discipline means boundaries. There's a boundary round sociology and, whatever happens outside, we must start with questions about balance within that boundary. If the argument is that sociology can be left-wing because political science is right-wing, that is the beginning of the end for both disciplines.

PM: Why are these 'principles of scholarship' so important?

DM: They are a fundamental strand of civilisation. In defending scholarship, we are also in part defending political democracy.

PM: Is it really that important? There aren't many people involved, after all.

DM: Sociology is big and it's growing, and it will continue to do so. The sociological way of thinking has become central to how many people make sense of their lives. The media is permeated with it.

PM: How would you summarise your views? Is it just a question of correcting some fairly simple weaknesses in teaching and in textbooks?

DM: No. It's deeper than that. Much of our basic sociological thinking has been shaped in such a way that it is impossible to come up with arguments and accounts that are genuinely liberal. In a sense, sociology, as it is, is incompatible with a way of thinking which is even half-way positive about capitalism. The errors go back a long way, as far as Herbert Spencer, and right through to Talcott Parsons.

What is exciting is that these conceptual problems are yielding to questions. We can take sociology forward by talking and arguing together.

30 OCTOBER 1987

FURTHER READING

Marsland, D. (1987) *Bias against Business* (Educational Research Trust).
Marsland, D. (1987) *Seeds of Bankruptcy* (Pickwick Books).

* Professor David Marsland is Reader in Social Science at the West London Institute of Higher Education.

69

All Change

> ## *Sociology in the 1990s*

PAT MCNEILL: Dr Bulmer, you have been concerned with sociological research in the UK for twenty years. How has the pattern of research changed over that time?

MARTIN BULMER:* First, there is much more research being done today than 20 years ago, whether by academics, by government, or by independent research institutes. Secondly, there has been a movement away from the two classical models of British social research. These were, on the one hand, the anthropological community studies of the 1950s, and on the other hand social surveys, typically about some aspect of social stratification. There is now more interest in other methods of research, particularly the ethnographic, as well as increasing interest in secondary data such as personal documents and official statistics. There have been developments in methods of content analysis, and in the storage, manipulation and retrieval of data using new technology. Sociologists are also making more use of methods developed by historians.

Thirdly, there is the growth of inter-disciplinary research centres in which sociologists are involved, such as the Welfare State programme at the London School of Economics, the Social Policy Research Unit at York, or the new Inter-disciplinary Research Centre at Essex. There is much more diversity of methods. This is also true within particular research studies, where people are more willing to use multiple and complementary methods.

PM: Which specialist areas are now the most active in research terms?

MB: There are several. Stratification, for example, has always been a major area for research, and the contemporary inheritors of that tradition are studies of economic life and the labour market, such as Ray Pahl's 'Divisions of Labour'. These studies still tend to focus on the working class rather than the middle class.

Another major area is the sociology of health and illness. Those working here are very much involved in major policy issues, such as the Black Report and its follow-up study 'The Health Divide'. This work points to the continuing importance of social class as an important factor in explaining health inequalities.

Development studies attract a lot of attention. That too is becoming almost a separate field involving economists, anthropologists and political scientists as well as sociologists. The sociology of culture, in the wider sense, is another growth area, including literary materials, film and television. An example is the 'Bad News' studies of TV news from Glasgow.

Another expanding field is historical sociology. The general public is much more aware of history than of sociology, and now the two disciplines are coming closer together, with sociologists doing historical work and with history becoming more sociological.

PM: What is the current position on funding for research?

MB: The crisis in university funding has affected the social sciences quite severely. It has led both to the early retirement of a generation of British sociologists and also to a near-freeze on the recruitment of young sociologists. Teachers of sociology have seen their opportunities for personal research decrease and research grants have become more difficult to get, whether from research councils or charitable sources such as Leverhulme, Rowntree or Nuffield.

But it is important not to forget government-funded research. The Department of Health funds several million pounds of research into health and the personal social services. The Department of Employment has an annual budget of about a million pounds for research on the labour market, and the Home Office has a similar research budget largely to do with crime. The Office of Population Censuses and Surveys does both one-off surveys and repeated surveys like the General Household Survey, which are very valuable for secondary analysis. All of these studies are designed to answer questions of interest to government.

PM: How much is choice of topic or research design affected by levels of funding?

MB: The Economic and Social Research Council is more oriented towards basic social science research, and government departments towards applied research. But both types are being done, and they use a variety of methods. What determines your chance of funding is the topic you are working on rather than the way you approach it. For example, a topic like the elderly, or crime, in which there is a direct policy interest, is more likely to attract funding than a topic like 'Changes in working-class culture'.

PM: In some cases, such as football hooliganism, the policy interest is in control, isn't it?

MB: Yes, but that gives sociologists an opportunity. For example, research like Eric Dunning's at Leicester can show that the problem is much more complex than it appears, and that many of the control measures proposed by government are not appropriate. Similarly, the theory of the short, sharp shock for young offenders was not supported by research.

PM: What of the future for sociology in the 1990s?

MB: I'm more optimistic than some people. Sociology can offer ways of understanding society that are not available from other sources, such as journalists, however well-informed and perceptive they are. A sociologist is trying to interpret social behaviour within a theoretical framework and make general statements which will help make sense of behaviour in a particular setting. I think many more people are beginning to recognise that potential.

But I also believe that sociologists need to pay more attention to their audiences. Some are very good at communicating to a wide public, but too many only address other sociologists. History has always had both academic and popular historians who can project their work to a wider audience. We need more people like that in sociology.

15 DECEMBER 1989

Discussion Topic

What are the main differences between a politician's and a sociologist's approach to a problem such as football hooliganism?

* Martin Bulmer is Reader in Social Administration at the London School of Economics.

Index

The numbers in this index refer to the articles rather than to the pages of the book.

The numbers in heavy type denote that the article in question is substantially about the index item.

Thus 'Age' **22**, 33, 51 means that Article 22 takes 'Age' as its central theme, whereas there is only a passing reference or a short discussion of 'Age' in Articles 33 and 51.